W9-DCL-857

Communication Behavior and Experiments

Communication Behavior and Experiments: A Scientific Approach

R. Wayne Pace
University of New Mexico

Robert R. Boren
Boise State University

Brent D. Peterson
Brigham Young University

Wadsworth Publishing Company, Inc.
Belmont, California

We would like to dedicate this book to our parents:

Ralph W. Pace
Elda F. Pace

Gilbert R. Boren
Olive M. Boren

Dan W. Peterson
Maxine Peterson

Designer: Ann Wilkinson

© 1975 by Wadsworth Publishing Company, Inc., Belmont, California 94002. All rights reserved. No part of this book may be reproduced, stored in a retrieval system or transcribed, in any form or by any means, electronic, mechanical, photocopying, recording or otherwise, without the prior written permission of the publisher.

ISBN 0-534-00404-0

L. C. Cat. Card No. 74-20346

Printed in the United States of America

1 2 3 4 5 6 7 8 9 10 — 79 78 77 76 75

Communication Behavior

R. Wayne Pace

Robert R. Boren

Brent D. Peterson

Preface

One cannot attend college in contemporary America, regardless of his or her chosen area of study, without coming into contact with what is called *science*. Also, regardless of discipline, students are always involved with *communication*. In fact, of all the social behaviors familiar to students, communication is probably the most fundamental. This book is an attempt to view *communication* from a scientific point of view. It is an attempt to present a selected body of communication principles that appear to have some basis in scientific information. This is *not* a book about how to communicate better, although the information and principles presented could be utilized to develop improved skills in communicating. Instead, the approach is to present information about communicating in terms of *if-then* propositions that have some basis in scientific study. These propositions suggest that *if* you behave in a particular way, *then* a reasonable probability exists that a specified consequence will occur.

However, neither instructor nor student should read this book believing he or she is discovering basic *laws* of human communicative behavior. If, as we believe, communication is *process*, then such absolute laws do not exist. However, man is a predicting animal, and his predictions vary in the probability of their accuracy. Neither we nor the field of communication are much beyond stating some rather preliminary predictions—predictions that are really guesses deserving to be put to the test. However, the first steps in building a scientific principle consist of making guesses about what might happen, and then formulating ways of finding out what in fact does happen and determining the probability of its repetition in the future.

In spite of the claims of some, the method of science harbors neither mystery nor magic. It simply demands that data be gathered with the minimum of bias and preconceived notions and that conclusions be drawn from this data in a reasonable manner. Following the method of science, the same essential observational or experimental procedures should yield the same essential information whether one person or another follows those procedures. The scientific method does demand that guesses be tested, checked, retested, and rechecked by further empirical procedures. Such guesses are ever changing things and are actually important only insofar as they help interpret and explain communicative behavior. It is this ability to change constantly that provides science with its strength. New, perhaps more accurate explanations of communicative behavior eventually replace older, perhaps less accurate explanations and, hopefully, increase the probability that our predictions about the consequences that occur from communication might be accurate.

This book consists of two sections, *Communication Behavior* and *Communication Experiments*. The chapters in the first section, *Communication Behavior,* consider relationships, messages, information diffusion, and achieving change. In this section of the book, some predictive propositions that appear to be supported by existing scientific research are discussed. A sample of supporting research for each proposition is reviewed and at least one representative study is abstracted. The second section, *Communication Experiments,* outlines twenty basic experiments, which students can carry out as a means of learning about scientific research and verifying or refuting some of the predictive propositions discussed in the first section. Step-by-step procedures for conducting these experiments are also provided.

The genesis of a book of this sort lies in the inspiration of special people during difficult times. The persistent and gentle guidance of W. Charles Redding, scholar, advisor, provocateur, and Director of the Communication Research Center, Purdue University, shaped and motivated the desire to try. The genial, but rigorous prodding of Carl H. Weaver, listening scientist, helpful responder, and friend, of Ohio University, stirred the early beginnings of our communication point of view. The persistent inquiries and challenges of many students forced us to examine constantly that which we thought and taught.

The authors are deeply indebted to the scientists of the past who were sufficiently interested in communicative behavior to make some guesses and put them to a test. From this fund of information which they generated, we have drawn freely in building this book. We seek to give them full credit wherever possible.

We wish to acknowledge the insightful perceptions and thoughtful comments of reviewers of the manuscript—Kenneth Frandsen of Pennsylvania State University, Cal Hylton of San Jose State University, Charles Petrie of the State University of New York at Buffalo, and Noel White of Eastern Washington State University.

We also express our gratitude to Rebecca Hayden, Communications Editor, Wadsworth Publishing Company, for her patience and long suffering and for her most useful editorial suggestions and support.

To our families, we once again and continuously express our love and appreciation for their communicativeness under trying conditions.

Finally, we are grateful to Gary Beckstrom, Gary Cook, and Mark Johnson, Brigham Young University, for their assistance with the index. We are also appreciative of the expert assistance provided by May Polivka, Secretary, Department of Speech Communication, University of New Mexico; Mary Ann Kline, Secretary, Department of Communication, Boise State University; and Anette Bradford, Speech Communication Secretary, Brigham Young University, in typing various parts of the manuscript and managing affairs so as to allow us to put it all together.

RWP   RRB   BDP

Contents

See also the Contents for *Communication Experiments* in the section following the colored divider.

Part 2
Messages

Chapter 3
Message Reception and Processing   **37**

Chapter 4
Message Preparation and Presentation   **48**

Part 3
Information Diffusion

Chapter 5
Face-to-Face Groups   **63**

Chapter 6
Social Groups   **70**

Prethoughts

Communicology: A Body of Knowledge

Many books have been written about human communication. Most have focused on improving skills in human communication, including public speaking, debate, group discussion, journalism, and broadcasting. This book allows you to embark upon a relatively new learning experience. Most of you may, at least initially, even wonder about the authors' approach and subject matter. For many, this may be your first experience with a book that acknowledges and advances a field called *communicology*. However, scholars from diverse disciplines are engaged in research and writing about the tenets of communicology and, on occasion, a few have even referred to such a body of knowledge (Knower, 1967; Applbaum and others, 1973).

As President of the International Communication Association, R. Wayne Pace (1970) observed that those involved in the scientific study of communicative behavior might rightly be called *communicologists*. Likewise, those applying the knowledge generated by communicologists might be legitimately called *communicators*.

Communicative behavior is studied because it contributes to improving communication skills. Communicology, however, represents a body of knowledge that helps us to *understand and predict*, among other things, how people will react to certain kinds of messages, and to explain why people behave as they do. Such information can be useful in making desirable changes in the way we communicate with others. You may even choose to study communication simply to know what happens when people attempt to communicate.

Communicology consists of a number of more or less verified statements about relationships among the variables of human communication. These statements, which constitute our current knowledge of communicative processes, have been created and accumulated, often painstakingly, over long periods of time. They have been tested, more or less vigorously, by scholars and practitioners in laboratories and in the marketplace of human interaction.

The result has been a rapid expansion in the number of studies about communicating as an experience, about the features and elements of a communicative situation.

1

These studies have not only added immensely to our understanding of communicative processes but have also complicated our efforts to make meaningful analyses and presentations about what communicology means. Such available information from broad fields like psychology, sociology, biology, anthropology, psychiatry, linguistics, speech, and philosophy—and from specialized areas like neuropsychology, cognition, learning, information processing, creative thinking, organization theory, political behavior, psychophysiology, ethnography, and electrical engineering—can indeed be overwhelming.

Sometimes we discover that earlier studies and conclusions have not withstood the test of either the laboratory or practical application. When that happens we should modify what we say about communication by substituting more accurate generalizations about what occurs when people communicate. Through constant scientific and pragmatic evaluation, we can discard whatever fails to ring true. In this way each new generation can be assured that its knowledge in the area is reasonably current and accurate.

Unfortunately, an introductory book can neither cover all the generalizations about the field of communication nor provide all the empirical data supporting them. Thus, our presentation will cover only what seem to be basic, relevant, and widely applicable propositions for understanding human communicative behavior. Since the results must necessarily be quite selective and often limited in their applicability, mastering the contents of this book will not make you a communication specialist. That goal constitutes a lifelong career. Since the topics are reasonably diverse, a diligent and interested person will find himself or herself adequately prepared to explore more specialized approaches to communicology. Above all, we will explore information about communicative behavior rooted in the social and behavioral sciences.

Often the term "science" connotes specialized and technical analyses of physical and biological phenomena. A science of communication, following that line of thought, would consist of detailed tests of the fine points of human speech production, auditory perception, psychophysiological responses in human information processing, structural analyses of grammars and other coding and linguistic features of language behavior, as well as the functioning of the neuropsychological dimensions of language acquisition. George Miller (1951) approaches his "scientific and psychological introduction" to communication in just that way. Beginning with a summary of experimental research on human vocalization and acoustics, the book explains such topics as speech perception, relative frequencies of verbal elements, information, noise and redundancy, verbal diversification and type-token ratios, verbal behavior of children, and abstraction and concept formation. The final chapter is devoted to the social processes of communication, including rumor transmission in small and large groups. On the other hand, Wilbur Schramm (1963) brings together the approaches of a number of well-known specialists on topics such as the social effects of mass communication, the theory of cognitive dissonance, semantic space, attitude change processes, the diffusion of new ideas, and teaching machines and instruction. Although both books purport to represent "scientific" introductions to communicative processes, they deal with quite different aspects of human communication.

Like Miller and Schramm, we will delineate the parameters of the field with which we will be directly concerned, dealing only with a portion of the knowledge implied by the scope of communicology.

Definition of Communicology

Communicology may be defined as a body of scientific information about human interaction as it is mediated by message systems. Messages represent a person's interpretations of the actions, statements, and behaviors of other people, events, and objects. Actions that are not interpreted do not qualify as messages, which by our definition serve as intermediary agencies between human beings and influence human interaction. When two or more people interact with one another, they respond to each other as message sources. If we talk about messages designed to evoke specific responses, we mean that auditory and visual (and sometimes olfactory, gustatory, and tactile) sensations are deliberately structured so they will be interpreted in the desired way. Much of what we need to learn about communicative behavior has to do with how people respond to these particular arrangements of stimuli (sounds, pictures, written and oral language, for example). Communicologists have a legitimate interest in all aspects of the world that influence the development and processing of messages, but our concern will be with the ways in which human beings create and interpret messages.

A scientific introduction to communication implies a slightly broader focus than a text about a particular communicative form. Differences between speech communication, interpersonal communication, human communication, oral communication, written communication, verbal communication, and vocal communication rest more on what aspect of the communicative process is being emphasized than in substantive differences in content. Although all analyses in this area must deal with the phenomena of communicating, some scientists may wish to examine primarily vocal symbols while others study primarily visual symbols. Some may focus entirely on the preparation and presentation of messages over electronic media, including visual and vocal (audio and visual) symbols. Some may prefer to study *written* documents, such as newspapers, poetry, or essays (some speeches are written so as to represent vocal messagess recorded in visual symbols), which involve nonvocal symbols more than vocal symbols.

For practical reasons we are concerned with messages created with, primarily, vocal and verbal symbols. The most impelling implication of this conception is that *communication* represents a wholly human activity that combines not only vocal utterances but also the accompanying nonverbal behavior into a single source of sensations for generating messages in other people. Communication behavior, then, is more than merely making vocalizations; it consists of interpreting —assigning meaning to—people, events, and objects so as to create messages. Communication, thus, represents the central activity of human beings: the creation of and response to messages, their own and others.

Human interaction always occurs in some type of relationship; that is, people relate to one another on a one-to-one basis, or as a group, an audience, a society, or an organization. They may even relate to themselves on a "self-1 to self-2" basis. Messages function to mediate human interaction. It is the creation of similar messages among individuals that allows a group to form and to be sustained. Messages, on the other hand, are affected by one's perceptions. If a relationship is interpreted, for example, as somewhat distant, cold, and formal, a different kind of message will no doubt occur than if the relationship is interpreted as being close, warm, and informal. Other relationships are both an antecedent and a consequent of particular message systems.

Human behavior is influenced, modified, and changed by means of the messages people create inside themselves. Both messages and relationships can be analyzed from what they are designed to accomplish. As a structural architect designs a building, messages are designed by communication "architects." As buildings are aesthetically and functionally sound, so messages must appeal to the artistic sense and to the pragmatic concerns of communicators. It is possible to consider messages by looking at the information they generate and/or the changes that occur from exposure to them. We can ask questions like these: "How does one disseminate information most effectively to a large audience of people?" Or "What kinds of changes occur in the designed message as it is disseminated through chains of individuals?" Or "What changes occur in the behavior of individuals and their relationship to others as a consequence of certain types of messages?"

The major sections of this book, therefore, concern *relationships, messages, information diffusion,* and *change.* Scientific data are available in varying degrees on many propositions in each area. We are not attempting a thorough and routine treatment of all of the information about communication. We are, however, providing a framework upon which you may build a firm structure of knowledge of communicative events in each of these four areas.

Communicology as Knowledge Rather Than Practice

In most scientific fields, specialists have developed competencies in two directions: (1) by acquiring knowledge about the behaviors in question and (2) by acquiring abilities to perform the behaviors in question. The latter often assumes a competence in the former, but they represent distinctly different types of competencies. Skills of knowledge acquisition differ sharply from skills of performance. Performers should be able to benefit from the knowledge acquired. Scholar–scientists have quite different objectives in mind from practitioner–therapists when studying the same body of knowledge.

The communicologist (scholar–scientist) is interested chiefly in knowing and discovering the *what* and *why* of communicative processes and behavior that will help create knowledge about communicative events. On the other hand, the communicator (practitioner–therapist) is professionally interested only in the knowledge that will assist him in behaving more effectively toward others or helping them to interact or perform more skillfully. This means his knowledge must be practical or immediately useful in working with people.

Since communicology is a field of knowledge, the communicologist's main responsibility is to develop an accurate body of statements about communicative behavior. The use of this knowledge is the province of the communicator, who, though he does not merit the title of communicologist, certainly communicates in one way or another. Communicators may be found functioning as advertisers, public speakers, counselors, teachers, managers, public relations advisors, writers or authors, journalists, marketing consultants, television producer–directors, instructional materials specialists, or salespeople. The list could be expanded but this sampling may be illustrative. The main point is that the body of knowledge about communicative behavior has practical value but is usually put into use by people other than communicologists. To avoid the criticism, however, of being totally "ivory-towered" in our approach, we have systematically incorporated sections on how this knowledge may be used in communicating. Thus, you may sense some of the satisfactions to be derived from applying these principles in improving communication skills.

A scientific perspective seems to lead people quite naturally to wonder about the truthfulness of many of our everyday, routine skills. Is it best, for example, to smile and shake another person's hand vigorously when you want him to help you do something? Is it best to say "Yes, I certainly think you are right, but wouldn't it be better to . . ." when you want to change someone's mind? Is it best to threaten people when you want them to do what you ask? A communicologist wonders about the effectiveness of different kinds of messages; he is curious about how messages affect different relationships, about what affects the development of different kinds of messages, as well as how people process and respond to messages.

We will have accomplished a major objective if you become inquisitive about communicative behavior in general—your own, that of others, and the two in relationship to each other. Naturally, we would like you to go beyond just developing an inquisitive attitude about communication. We would like you to learn something about the science of communication itself and to do some type of scientific study of communicative processes to expand your own knowledge (and possibly that of others) of communication.

Communicology in Relation to Other Social and Behavioral Sciences

Communicology is, of course, not the only science concerned with human behavior. Anthropology, political science, psychology, and sociology are disciplines that also provide information about human behavior. Information about communication, since it represents a central, if not the fundamental, social process, comes from all the social and behavioral sciences. Someone in each discipline formally classified under social and behavioral sciences has at one time or another focused on communicative behavior. Introductory textbooks in psychology, sociology, political science, and anthropology almost universally devote some space to a discussion of communication. In much the same way, introductory textbooks in communicology relate the study of psychology, sociology, anthropology, and political science to communication. Only communicology, however, makes the study of communicative behavior its central concern. This means that books about communicology draw upon studies of communicative behavior by individuals who not only have a deep, abiding interest in human behavior in general but who, from time to time, have focused their attention directly on communication.

As an individual perhaps being introduced to this field of study for the first time, you may be surprised, then dismayed at the varied credentials of the individuals who have contributed to knowledge about communication. For example, the September 1972 issue of *Scientific American* was devoted entirely to communication. Contributors were identified as professors of electrical engineering, molecular biology, zoology, general linguistics, history of the classical tradition, electronic engineering, communications, and law. Others were associated with a data-communication technology laboratory, a communications research corporation, and a telephone and telegraph corporation. Few if any of the contributors were obviously identified with the social science and behavioral disciplines as discussed above. The meaning of this is not obvious, but one striking implication is that many people find knowledge about human communication useful. In the case of those involved in the technology of communication (engineers, data processors, and telephone–telegraph technologists), an understanding of how human beings communicate may be crucial; the creation of data-processing devices and telephone equipment may depend quite directly on the demands of the human information processor.

The overriding implication for most of us is that knowledge about communicative processes may emerge from almost any discipline. The primary sources are, naturally, the social sciences, especially those disciplines that study human behavior in general. As an inquiring individual, you should be ready to investigate and incorporate findings about human communication from any source. Be prepared to ask these questions: "Are the data scientifically sound?" and "What do the results contribute to an understanding of human communication?"

Methods of Scientific
Research in Communication

To understand questions like the above and to determine the accuracy of a theory or to change it to approximate reality more accurately, communicologists use experiments. What then is an experiment? Cattell (1966) suggests a definition of experiment that seems quite useful:

An experiment is a recording of observations, quantitative or qualitative, made by defined and recorded operations and in defined conditions, followed by examination of the data by appropriate statistical and mathematical rules, for the existence of significant relationships.

This definition is especially useful for communicologists because it provides for observing communicative behavior and for examining data or information collected by our observations. It also includes the *observation and measurement* of human behavior under conditions that occur naturally (field situations) as well as in the laboratory.

For years communicologists have attempted to differentiate between the types of experiments done in communication. They have generally classified experiments as (1) field studies or (2) laboratory studies. However, experiments in communication do not seem to fall neatly into these two categories. Both W. Charles Redding and Gerald R. Miller (in Emmert and Brooks, 1970) indicate that these two kinds of experiments are probably on the ends of a continuum with a variety of other experiments falling in between. Isaac and Michael (1971) express similar feelings about field and laboratory studies. They feel that experiments can be classified into at

6

least nine categories more representative of the continuum of kinds of experiments than field and laboratory studies alone. They stress that, although these nine categories are overlapping and arbitrary, they seem to represent a useful grouping of alternative experimental situations that can be used in discovering facts through the communication process. Even though Isaac and Michael apply these nine categories to educational research, we have taken the liberty to generalize their classifications to studies in communication.

As you examine these categories, keep in mind that the communicologist should have identified and/or asked the questions to be answered by the research before attempting to classify the kind of investigation. These classifications or research designs help refine an approach to the problem, as well as clarify what methods should be used and what strategies would be most effective in answering the questions posed by the study. In other words, the kinds of communicative questions the communicologist asks will determine which of the following methods he or she will use. The nine experimental methods, their purposes, and examples of how each is used include:

1. Historical Method   This method reconstructs the past in an objective and accurate manner. Often, a specific hypothesis is evaluated on the basis of the reconstructed past. This method might be used in (1) a study reconstructing practices in the teaching of communication in the United States during the past 50 years; (2) a study tracing the approach to the study of interpersonal communication since the 1950s; (3) a study testing the hypothesis that Aristotle is not the author of all parts of *The Rhetoric*.

2. Descriptive Method   The descriptive method gains systematic information about a situation or an area of interest and describes it factually and accurately. Some examples of this method might be population census studies, public opinion surveys, fact-finding surveys, status studies, task-analysis studies, questionnaire and interview studies, observation studies, job descriptions, surveys of a body literature, documentary analyses, critical incident reports, test-score analyses, and normative data.

3. Developmental Method   This method develops information about patterns and sequences of growth and/or change as a function of time. This method might be used in (1) a study following a sample of 200 speech communication students through a given semester to analyze their growth as interpersonal communicators; (2) a study investigating changing communicative patterns by sampling groups of people at a number of different age levels; (3) a trend study projecting the need or lack of need for future communication training as a result of past trends and estimates.

4. Case and Field Method   This method gathers information about the background, current status, and environmental interactions of a given social unit such as an individual, a group, an institution, or a community. Some examples for using this method might be (1) the case history of an extremely successful personnel manager who seems to be an effective communicator; (2) an intensive study of communicative patterns of students who have had transactional analysis training; (3) an intensive study of the communication patterns within a business organization.

5. Correlation Method   This method is used to gain information about the extent to which variations in one factor correspond with variations in one or more other factors based on correlation coefficients. This method might be used in (1) a study investigating relationships between listening comprehension and intelligence tests; (2) a factor-analytic study of aspects of speaker credibility; (3) a study for predicting success in college based on correlations between college grades and participation in high school debate.

6. Causal–Comparative or "Ex Post Facto" Method   This method attempts to discover information about possible cause-and-effect relationships by observing some existing consequences and searching back through the data for plausible causal factors. This method might be used for (1) identifying factors related to effective human communication in a particular industrial organization by evaluating its communication over the past ten years; (2) investigating similarities and differences between such groups as smokers and nonsmokers, readers and nonreaders, or effective and noneffective communicators using data that are already on file.

7. True Experimental Method   This method searches for information about possible cause-and-effect relationships by exposing at least one experimental group to one or more treatment conditions and comparing the results with one or more control groups not receiving the treatment (random assignment being essential). This method might be used for (1) investigating the effectiveness of three methods of teaching interpersonal communication to college freshmen—students and instructors being randomly assigned to groups and methods; (2) investigating the persuasive effects of two women's liberation speeches, one pro and one con, on college men, who are randomly assigned to groups and the two speaking situations, as well as on a control group, who hear neither of the speeches.

8. Quasi-Experimental Method   This method looks for information by approximating the conditions of the true experiment in a setting that does not allow the control and/or manipulation of all relevant variables. The researcher should be aware of the compromises he is making and what limitations they place on the study when he uses this method. An example in which this method might be applied is in an organizational study for determining which of two new techniques of communication is better for passing information along in two organizations. Most so-called field experiments fall under this method.

9. Action Method   This method is used to develop new skills or new approaches and solves problems with direct application to the classroom or other settings. Some examples in which this method might be used are (1) an in-service training program to help teachers develop new skills in facilitating class discussions or in experimenting with new approaches to teaching interpersonal communication and (2) a program to develop more effective communicative techniques for industrial interviewers.

As we review the various kinds of scientific experiments presented in later chapters, we will discover the full or partial use of each of these nine experimental methods. By keeping these methods in mind, we will have a better understanding of what kinds of information the communicologist is trying to gain with each experiment.

At this point it is important for us to realize that the selection of an experimental method or design is important, but its value depends on how well it measures up to established scientific standards of excellence. Pitfalls, sources of contamination, and numerous invalidating factors abound to challenge the findings and interpretations reported in any study. The most effective insurance against unwitting errors is sound, thorough planning that foresees problems and makes acceptable allowances where unavoidable difficulties exist. As we review the experiments that follow, we should try to determine if proper research methods were selected or if other pitfalls are detectable. None of these experiments are perfect, since all have problems limiting the reliability and validity of the information obtained.

Why Study Communicology?

Since it is obvious that reading and studying one book can only scratch the surface in the broad field of communication, an indication of what aspects we plan to discuss is essential. In summary form, our purposes, along with limiting factors, are the following:

1. *To familiarize students with a scientific perspective toward communicative behavior.* We have made some preliminary attempts to state a communicology point of view, but it will be made more explicit in succeeding chapters. At least from this familiarization we hope a greater sensitivity to both the strengths and weaknesses of scientific information about human communication will evolve. Ultimately, we hope to attract more individuals to a serious study of the scientific knowledge we have of communication so they can produce more accurate predictions by testing and revising present generalizations. The importance of human communication to social processes in general makes the information of communicology an exciting and important contribution to knowledge.

2. *To state in the form of generalizations some of the information created by communicologists about four broad areas of concern:* relationships, messages, the diffusion of information, and achieving change. The emphasis will be primarily upon consequences. Generalizations, for example, will often be phrased as "if-then" propositions, in which effects will be postulated as the result of certain conditions. Important variables such as source, message, channel, receiver, content, setting, and media will be systematically treated in chapters relevant to these four broad areas of concern.

Of the literally thousands of potential generalizations, propositions, and hypotheses that could be stated, we have selected those that, in our view, seem to be among those basic to understanding human communication. Many of the propositions could be labeled as essentially rhetorical in origin and focus, others appear to be primarily interpersonal or related to a small group, while still others seem to be derived from mass communication sources. The propositions chosen argue for a common thread grounded in the basic concept of communicology in which distinctions between rhetoric, mass communication, and interpersonal communication disappear. This is not an introduction to some particular part of the theory and/or practice of human communication but a broadly based introduction to many aspects of the field. In addition, the skills and practices of human communication are introduced as *implications* derived from the research.

3. *To describe and illustrate research methods, procedures, and techniques appropriate to communicology.* Through various means we shall attempt to demonstrate how communicologists gather and interpret scientific information. Although this is *not* a textbook on research methods, you should learn, through the use of abstracts and discussions of philosophy and data, how to assemble information so as to develop more accurate predictions about human communicative behavior.

4. *To acquaint students with the basic technical vocabulary of communicology.* Merely learning to spell and repeat certain words, however, is not the goal; the emphasis, instead, is upon being able to explain what the words stand for and to relate them to the concepts and behavior. Although communicology, like other sciences, has many technical terms that are used exclusively by scientists in the field, an abundance of communication terms have popular meanings that may be quite different from the scientific ones. Since the relationship of a word to what it represents is arbitrary (a basic principle of communicology), we often invent different relationships between words and things. We choose to have widely known words refer to very specific experiences; otherwise, words begin to refer to different experiences than initially intended. This means we need to *operationalize* (a scientific concept) our meanings in order to increase the probabilities of similar responses. In other words, we must learn to specify what our words mean. Part of the task of scholarship in any field of study is learning its special language so we can communicate its ideas and concepts. Like other fields, communicology uses the terms of science, thus, if you have studied biology or physics, you will find a great many words familiar to you. However, some terms, such as modes, codes, signs and symbols, may be less familiar.

This book is about communicology. Contemporary communicology represents a body of knowledge about human communication rather than a skill or set of skills useful in practicing human communication. That knowledge consists primarily of generalizations derived from careful observations of people, behavior, objects, and events. Particular kinds of behaviors and events observed consist primarily of relationships between people in which messages mediate behavior and/or in which change or diffusion of information are the major concerns of those involved. Although communicology is only one of the many sciences concerned with understanding human behavior, it is the only social science that makes communicative behavior its primary emphasis. Full exposure to the knowledge of communicology may stimulate an inquisitive attitude and encourage interested individuals to explore the field of communicative study in greater depth.

The chapters that follow will not only take up a variety of propositions dealing with communicative relationships but will also discuss some of the scientific research completed in the areas of each. Hopefully, they will provide an introduction to human communication behavior that will help us create a framework upon which we can build further knowledge about communication.

Background Readings

Research on communication propositions is gradually being summarized and synthesized into essays and books so as to be more easily available to scholars in the field. Beyond introductory textbooks, these unique publications contribute to the specialized knowledge about communication and assist in the evolution of a communicology.

Barker, Larry L., and Robert J. Kibler, eds., *Speech Communication Behavior: Perspectives and Principles* (Englewood Cliffs, N. J.: Prentice-Hall, 1971). Contains original essays summarizing research on important topics such as acquisition and performance of communication behaviors, human information processing and diffusion, and persuasion. It represents a status report on some selected perspectives concerning communication processes.

Berelson, Bernard, and Gary A. Steiner, *Human Behavior: An Inventory of Scientific Findings* (New York: Harcourt Brace Jovanovich, 1964). This book represents an inventory or catalog of the state of scientific knowledge about human behavior. It presents an itemization of generalizations about human behavior and a nontechnical explanation of what is known about each one. Topics such as perceiving, learning and thinking, motivation, face-to-face relations, organizations, ethnic relations, mass communication, and opinions, attitudes, and beliefs are covered.

Kline, F. Gerald, and Phillip J. Tichenor, eds., *Current Perspectives in Mass Communication Research* (Beverly Hills, Calif.: Sage Publications, 1972). Summarizes research being done in schools of mass communication and journalism on such topics as gatekeeping, information diffusion, socialization, political campaigns, the communication environment of the urban poor, and the environment and communication.

Martin, Howard H., and Kenneth E. Andersen, eds., *Speech Communication: Analysis and Readings* (Boston: Allyn and Bacon, 1968). This book provides an exposure to some of the research on communication through syntheses and some original essays. Tentative generalizations are listed at the ends of each chapter that help to organize knowledge about communication processes.

Ried, Paul E., ed., *The Frontiers in Experimental Speech-Communication Research* (Syracuse, N. Y.: Syracuse University Press, 1966). This monograph consists of the proceedings of the First Conference in Speech Education and Experimental Speech Research held at Syracuse University. It contains synthesizing essays on the state of experimental communication research, communication in education settings, and human communication in business and industry.

Thompson, Wayne N., *Quantitative Research in Public Address and Communication* (New York: Random House, 1967). This volume summarizes and evaluates quantitative research in speech as published in journals of the Speech Communication Association, regional speech communication associations, and the *Journal of Communication*. Published research is abstracted and summarized under propositions. A brief critique is offered commenting on the quality of the research.

Part 1
Relationships

Alfred Korzybski (1948) once commented that no object exists in absolute isolation. He noted: "If there is no such thing as an absolutely isolated object, then at least we have two objects, and we shall always discover some relation between them, depending on our interests, ingenuity, and whatnot. Obviously, for a man to speak about anything at all, *always* presupposes two objects, at least; namely, the object spoken about and the speaker. And so, a *relation* between the two is always present."

When two or more people attempt to communicate with one another, a relationship exists between them. This relationship represents some type of connection between the individuals involved. To be connected or to have some connection with an individual implies being joined, fastened, bound, or united with him or her. It also implies a particular type of connection, one involving meaning, understanding, and feeling.

As we use the terms, relations exist between things, but *relationships* exist only between people. While a relation implies a connection between objects or even between two people, a relationship suggests an *intimate* connection involving feelings—that is, some type of emotional "connection" between people that is beyond a simple relation. John Powell (1969) clearly identifies the importance of relationships when he says, "What I am at any given moment in the process of my becoming a person will be determined by my relationships with those who love me or refuse to love me, with those whom I love or refuse to love." He also states: "It is certain that a relationship will be *only as good as its communication.*" Thus, relationships and communication depend upon each other for success.

Of primary importance in Chapter 1 is an analysis of what constitutes a desirable relationship. Desirability, of course, must be defined in terms of objectives. Hence, we shall look at relationships in terms of how they facilitate certain goals.

Chapter 2 will discuss methods and techniques for achieving more effective relationships. Some attempt will be made to formulate a set of propositions that may provide some guidelines for improving relationships. Of special interest are techniques of interpersonal effectiveness, including questions as to how to accept self and others, how to express feelings verbally and nonverbally, and how to listen and respond helpfully.

Together, Chapters 1 and 2 represent a unit on interpersonal relationships. Exploring these propositions early in the book and possibly early in your studies should not only provide information about communicating but also suggest ways of facilitating relationships among those with whom you are studying and learning.

1.1   An effective interpersonal relationship occurs when both parties have a direct, personal encounter and meet one another on a person-to-person basis.

1.2   An effective interpersonal relationship occurs when both parties experience and are able to communicate some significant aspects of an accurate empathic understanding of each other's private world.

1.3   An effective interpersonal relationship occurs when both parties express a warm, positive attitude toward each other.

1.4   An effective interpersonal relationship occurs when both parties express an accepting attitude (unconditional positive regard) toward each other regardless of the particular behavior of either person, at a particular moment.

1.5   An effective interpersonal relationship occurs when both parties perceive each other as maintaining an open and supportive climate.

1.6   An effective interpersonal relationship occurs when both parties exhibit trusting behavior and reinforce feelings of security in each other.

1.7   An effective interpersonal relationship occurs when both parties accept responsibility for misunderstandings.

Chapter 1
Interpersonal Dynamics

Communication with others most often occurs through face-to-face interaction, which is often referred to as *interpersonal communication.* At least four specific interpersonal relationships can be differentiated according to the number of individuals involved and the nature of the interaction. *Dyadic communication* occurs when two individuals interact with one another by each sending and receiving verbal and nonverbal messages. When the two-person dyad is expanded so that a message is relayed by a series of two-person interactions (e.g., Gregory to David to Michael to Stephen), in which each individual first interprets and then transmits a message to the next person in the chain, *serial communication* takes place. *Small group communication* occurs when from three to fifteen persons interact with one another in such a manner that each person influences and is influenced by the others. When the group expands beyond fifteen and gathers to listen to a single speaker, or even, perhaps, to several speakers, a new dimension has been added and *audience communication* occurs. Obviously, the precise number of individuals involved in small group or audience situations may vary considerably from the figures we have cited. However, these numbers provide some general guidelines for differentiating among those situations, although the nature of the interaction is the more significant feature for making distinctions.

In each of the relationships mentioned above the feature common to all of them is an interpersonal, person-to-person, face-to-face interaction. One individual establishes an emotional and cognitive connection with another or several others. Such interpersonal relationships are the focus of this chapter. We shall consider several predictive propositions representing statements about basic social relations, but these statements should not be interpreted as offering a general theory of interpersonal relationships.

Predictive Propositions

1.1 An effective interpersonal relationship occurs when both parties have a direct, personal encounter and meet one another on a person-to-person basis.

Phrased in another way this proposition says that *if* two people interact with one another on a deeply personal and honest level, then we can predict that an effective interpersonal relationship will follow from the interaction. The proposition, as stated, lacks many of the qualifying aspects important for rigorous scientific accuracy. For example, we lack a clear operational definition of such terms as "deeply personal and honest level" or "effective interpersonal relationship." As a result of these limitations, a great deal of ambiguity exists when you attempt to decide how one interacts with honesty. We need to point out these limitations in order to highlight the somewhat skeptical attitude with which predictions about interpersonal relationships should be examined. However, much research from the field of psychotherapy indicates that deeply personal and honest interaction will be predictably followed by positive and constructive interpersonal relationships. Much of the data demonstrating that people who meet one another on a person-to-person, rather than an impersonal, basis tend to develop effective interpersonal relationships comes from studies of therapeutic, clinical, and helping relationships. Let us look for a moment at a brief abstract of one such study.

Abstract

Morgan Worthy, Albert L. Geary, and Gay M. Kahn, "Self-Disclosure as an Exchange Process," *Journal of Personality and Social Psychology,* Vol. 13 (1969), No. 1, pp. 59–63.

Basically, this study by Worthy, Geary, and Kahn attempted to discover answers to two questions: (1) Does a person disclose intimate information to those from whom he receives intimate information? (2) Do people indicate greater liking for those from whom they receive intimate disclosure information?

In an effort to find answers to these questions, subjects were divided into groups of four and were given ten minutes in which to introduce themselves and get acquainted, after which a confidential rating was obtained from each indicating how much he or she liked the other three individuals. Subjects were then seated around a table and separated from each other by a wooden partition placed on the table. Then each person was provided with an identical set of seven questions numbered one through seven. The higher the number, the more intimate the question. Subjects exchanged notes requesting and providing answers to questions. Those who did not wish to answer a question indicated this by writing a zero on the note. The individuals who participated in the experiment were not allowed to answer the same question for more than one subject. This meant they had to choose which questions to answer and to whom to send questions. After a series of ten exchanges, the confidential measure of liking for each of the other individuals was again obtained.

The findings of this study indicate that more intimate initial disclosures were made to those who were initially better liked. In addition, more intimate information was disclosed to those who likewise disclosed intimate information. And, as one might expect, the final liking was higher for those who made the most intimate disclosures. In other words, the answer to each of the initial research questions was positive. Individuals did disclose intimate information to those from whom they received intimate information, and they did indicate greater liking for those from whom they received intimate disclosures.

■ This particular study lends credence to the original proposition that if two people interact with one another on a deeply personal level, then we can predict that an effective interpersonal relationship will follow. As the research implies, the more intimate the information, the more the disclosing individual was liked; and also the more intimate the information, the closer the relationship became. Perhaps, then, in communicating with others, close relationships can be developed by direct, personal interaction.

1.2 An effective interpersonal relationship occurs when both parties experience and are able to communicate some significant aspects of an accurate empathic understanding of each other's private world.

This proposition suggests that a positive relationship exists between *accurate empathy* and the development of effective interpersonal relationships. Empathy refers to an individual's ability to understand deeply the feelings, thoughts, and motives of another. If you have empathy with another person, you are mentally able to experience responses to a situation in a manner somewhat similar to the other person's experience. However, this proposition suggests that accurate empathy is not sufficient. In addition to being able to understand and share another's feelings, you must also be able to *communicate* that understanding to the other person. It is important that he understand that you understand. A study by Truax and others provides an example of research supporting this proposition.

Abstract

C. B. Truax, Ronald G. Wargo, Jerome D. Frank, and others, "Therapist Empathy, Genuineness, and Warmth and Patient Therapeutic Outcome," *Journal of Consulting Psychology,* Vol. 30 (1966), pp. 395–401.

The authors of this study were attempting to discover if patients receiving out-patient psychotherapy from psychiatrists offering high levels of accurate empathic understanding, genuineness, and nonpossessive warmth would show greater improvement than those receiving lower levels of these same qualities. In order to answer this question, 17 male and 23 female out-patients were assigned to four resident psychiatrists for four months. The therapists met the patients once a week for one-hour sessions that were tape recorded. The therapy provided was measured by three scales: the Accurate Empathy Scale, the Nonpossessive Warmth Scale, and the Therapist Genuineness Scale, which were developed at the University of Wisconsin's Psychiatric Institute. From each patient's set of recordings, six three-minute samples were excerpted for analysis on the basis of the three scales. In addition, both patients and therapists completed a "global improvement scale."

Interestingly, therapists who provided the highest levels of empathy during treatment also provided the highest levels of genuineness. Patients who received the highest levels of empathy, warmth, and genuineness combined tended to show significantly greater improvement on the overall global measures.

■ This proposition and the research relevant to it suggest that effective interpersonal relationships probably are encouraged when at least one party expresses empathy, which in turn also increases feelings of genuineness. Therefore, it seems reasonable to conclude that warm, genuine, and especially empathic communicators increase their probability of developing effective interpersonal relationships.

1.3   An effective interpersonal relationship occurs when both parties express a warm, positive attitude toward each other.

Warmth, as it is used in this proposition, refers to kindly feelings and friendliness toward another. It includes being sympathetically disposed and enthusiastic toward someone. Since most of us tend to like those who like us, an expression of warmth helps to produce positive feelings and attitudes in others and becomes an important way of building a climate conducive to effective relationships.

Abstract

David W. Johnson, "Effects of the Order of Expressing Warmth and Anger on the Actor and the Listener," *Journal of Counseling Psychology*, Vol. 18 (1971), pp. 571–578.

In this study Johnson attempts to determine the effect of expressing warmth or anger, singly or in different combinations, in initiating cooperation between the subjects involved.

Individuals in this study *engaged in* (actor) the expression of constant warmth, constant anger, anger followed by warmth, or warmth followed by anger, or they *listened* (listener) to a trained confederate express warmth and anger singly or in combination. The study found that the expression of anger followed by the expression of warmth tended to induce the most cooperation. Warmth also seemed to increase the attraction of the listener toward the actor. More cooperative behavior seemed to be induced in the listener when sustained warmth was expressed, while more cooperative behavior was induced in the actor when anger followed by warmth was expressed.

■ If the conclusions of this study are accurate, the implication is that expressing anger in combination with warmth is quite helpful in inducing public agreement. Apparently, expressions of warmth also tend to increase the quality of interpersonal relationships. Since warmth can improve both cooperation and interpersonal relationships, it seems clear that the development of skills that communicate feelings of warmth to other people may be very important in improving interpersonal interaction.

1.4 An effective interpersonal relationship occurs when both parties express an accepting attitude (unconditional positive regard) toward each other regardless of the particular behavior of either person at a particular moment.

To accept another person implies having a respect and liking for that person as a human being, as well as regarding that person as of value regardless of what he or she might be doing or feeling at the moment. Close personal relationships seem to occur when people are willing to accept one another, thus providing a psychologically safe environment in which each person is liked simply for being human. Though this acceptance implies supporting one another, it does not require that one person either agree or disagree with the other.

However, as with empathy, feelings of accepting others are not enough. These feelings must also be accurately communicated to the other person. Even if you honestly accept him, your attitude will not contribute to an effective interpersonal relationship unless he is able to recognize and understand your acceptance. The effectiveness of everyday relationships may well depend on expressing and recognizing attitudes of acceptance.

Abstract

Emanuel M. Berger, "The Relation between Expressed Acceptance of Self and Expressed Acceptance of Others," *Journal of Abnormal and Social Psychology*, Vol. 47 (1952), pp. 778–782.

In an attempt to determine the relationship between expressing acceptance of self and acceptance of others, Berger developed two scales of acceptance and administered them to a wide variety of subjects, including regular and evening college students, prisoners, stutterers, and adults in a YMCA class.

In finding a positive correlation between acceptance of self and acceptance of others, Berger also created theoretical definitions of accepting behavior that suggest why accepting individuals have a greater likelihood of developing effective interpersonal relationships than nonaccepting individuals. Characteristics of the accepting individual include the following:

Self-Accepting

1. Relies primarily on internalized values and standards rather than on external pressure as a guide for behavior
2. Has faith in his capacity to cope with life
3. Assumes responsibility for and accepts the consequences of his own behavior
4. Accepts praise or criticism from others objectively
5. Does not attempt to deny or distort any feelings, motives, limitations, abilities, or favorable qualities that he sees in himself but rather accepts all without self-condemnation
6. Considers himself a person of worth on an equal plane with other persons
7. Does not expect others to reject him whether he gives them reason to do so or not
8. Does not regard himself as totally different from others, strange, or generally abnormal in his reactions
9. Is not shy or self-conscious

Other Accepting

1. Does not reject, hate, or pass judgment against other persons when their behavior or standards seem to him to contradict his own
2. Does not attempt to dominate others
3. Does not attempt to assume responsibility for others
4. Does not deny the worth of others or their equality as persons with him
5. Shows a desire to serve others
6. Takes an active interest in others and

shows a desire to create satisfactory relationships with them

7. In attempting to advance his own welfare, he is careful not to infringe on the rights of others

■ As we can see, the qualities of acceptance—both self-acceptance and acceptance of others—are likely to create an atmosphere in which effective interpersonal relationships can develop.

1.5 An effective interpersonal relationship occurs when both parties perceive each other as maintaining an open and supportive climate.

Openness has to do with a person's willingness to consider new information and to share it with others. Individuals open to new information are also willing to share things about themselves with others. When ideas and feelings can be expressed candidly, an atmosphere of openness exists. However, when inappropriate things are shared or expressed, or when shared information seems to be used in harmful ways, defensiveness develops and openness decreases.

Supportiveness involves building and maintaining a person's sense of personal worth and importance. Supportive individuals are genuinely interested in the well-being of others and are friendly and helpful rather than hostile. Openness and supportiveness go hand-in-hand. In an open, supportive climate individuals seek to help one another and to develop a basis for understanding one another. As a result, there is less of a tendency for distortion to occur in the meanings communicated in the relationship.

Abstract

John W. Thibaut and John Coules, "The Role of Communication in the Reduction of Interpersonal Hostility," *Journal of Abnormal and Social Psychology,* Vol. 47 (1952), pp. 770–777.

This study was designed to answer one question: What effect does thwarting communication between an instigator of hostility and others have on the level of tension in their relationship? In the study one real and one confederate subject were allowed to exchange written messages about each other. The final message from the confederate to the actual subject was designed to induce hostility. Twenty-one subjects were permitted to communicate back to the instigator of hostility immediately after the offensive message, while the other 20 subjects were not permitted this final communication.

As you might expect, the subjects who were allowed to communicate back showed relatively more post-experimental friendliness toward the instigator of hostility than did those who were thwarted in such efforts. Asked if they would like to continue with the note writing, 40% of the thwarted communicators said no, while only 5% of those who were permitted to communicate back replied negatively.

■ It appears that a closed communicative relationship in which communication is thwarted tends to increase the level of hostility. Openness, of course, involves the willingness to have others talk back. When we are not willing, such a rejection tends to diminish the importance and worth of the other person and indicates a nonsupportive attitude. This will probably increase hostility rather than improve the interpersonal relationships, in which openness and supportiveness are basic to effective interaction.

1.6 An effective interpersonal relationship occurs when both parties exhibit trusting behavior and reinforce feelings of security in each other.

When we exhibit trusting behavior, we show confidence that the other person will not disappoint us. For example, if we trust an individual, we are confident that he or she will not respond to information we have disclosed in a way that will hurt our feelings or make us feel rejected. We also trust this person to be open and supportive in his or her communication. Generally, we tend to be trusted more by those to whom we exhibit trust. Conversely, if we feel that another does not trust us, we often do not trust him either.

Abstract

James L. Loomis, "Communication, the Development of Trust, and Cooperative Behavior," *Human Relations,* Vol. 12 (1959), pp. 305–315.

In this study Loomis attempted to discover the role of communication in establishing trust while at the same time considering how trust influences cooperative behavior. Subjects participated in a form of the prisoner's dilemma game, which is a situation in which each person is paired with a partner and has to choose between making decisions that increase his individual gain or increase to a lesser degree the total gain of both partners.

It appears, from this study, that the presence or absence of perceived trust determined the subject's choice of cooperative (joint gain) or uncooperative (personal gain) behavior. If the subject perceived trust in the relationship, he or she more often cooperated (behaved in a trustworthy manner) and did not attempt to doublecross the other person. If, on the other hand, the subject did not perceive

trust, he did not cooperate but, instead, behaved defensively. In those situations in which subjects communicated with one another, they were much more likely to perceive trusting relationships than were the noncommunicating subjects. Interestingly, the probability of perceiving trust increased as the level of communication increased.

■ Apparently a fairly clear relationship exists between degree of trust and cooperative behavior. This leads us to assume that cooperation requires the type of interpersonal relationship that comes from exhibiting trusting behavior and reinforcing feelings of security. To the extent that you are closed when others are trying to be open and self-disclosing, you will most likely not be trusted. Whenever you reject, ridicule, or disrespect the response of another person, you will most likely not be trusted. On the other hand, statements of support, acceptance of what others say, and respect of others will tend to increase trust in the relationship and, ultimately, improve it.

1.7 An effective interpersonal relationship occurs when both parties accept responsibility for misunderstandings.

A major source of communication problems is the failure of one or both parties in a relationship to interpret accurately what the other means when he or she communicates. We are often not understood as we would like to be. When misunderstanding occurs and I claim it is your fault, I have just set the stage for a defensive, nontrusting response on your part. If, however, I suggest that both of us may have contributed to the misunderstanding and that we should work together to achieve a more accurate interpretation of the problem, then, perhaps, I have created a climate in which a trusting, understanding, and supportive relationship may develop. Whenever both of us can accept responsibility for decisions, we will usually be able to develop a cooperative relationship with a mutually high level of satisfaction. Effective interpersonal relationships are more often than not based upon this assumption of mutual acceptance of responsibility. When one of us feels that he knows what is best for both of us, mutual responsibility gives way to control. Hostility and defensiveness evolve out of control and lead to a deterioration in the relationship.

Abstract

Irwin Katz, Judith Goldston, Melvin Cohen, and Solomon Stucker, "Need Satisfaction, Perception, and Cooperative Interaction in Married Couples," *Marriage and Family Living,* Vol. 25 (Feb. 1963), pp. 209–213.

Although this study focused directly on interaction of married couples, it also provides information applicable to other encounters between two people. Basically, the study attempted to determine whether or not marriage partners who experienced high satisfaction of their needs in their relationship were (1) more favorable in describing their spouses, (2) more acceptant of their spouse's suggestions when making judgments, (3) better able to coordinate their own motor responses with those of their spouses, and (4) more likely to confide in their spouses. In seeking answers to these questions, 59 young, childless volunteer couples completed three questionnaires:

1. One in which subjects rated the extent to which their spouses tended to satisfy or thwart psychological needs, such as affiliation, achievement, aggression, autonomy, deference, endurance, exhibition, dominance, nurturance, and succorance
2. One in which 20 self-disclosure items were grouped according to anxiety- and nonanxiety-producing characteristics
3. An 85-item adjective checklist on which subjects were asked to mark the 25 items most descriptive of self and the 25 most descriptive of the spouse

After completing the questionnaires, the subjects performed two tasks: first, a two-person coordination game and, then, an influence test of 50 problems. For the problem-solving task, subjects were placed in separate rooms and told to signal the answers they thought were correct. Husbands who experienced high levels of satisfaction of their needs described their wives more favorably on the checklist. High-satisfaction couples also scored significantly higher on the ball-spiral game. High-satisfaction husbands not only accepted the suggestions of their wives in solving problems more often but also made self-disclosures more often on anxiety topics.

■ Apparently, when a person perceives the other individual as providing satisfaction for his needs, he is able to interact more effectively. Thus, it is important in communicating to maintain a mutually satisfying and cooperative relationship. A major factor in such a relationship appears to be the acceptance on the part of both individuals of the responsibility for minimizing misunderstandings. To the extent that we are mutually willing to share responsibility, we are able to operate with feelings of high satisfaction of needs and thus are able to develop and maintain satisfying and cooperative relationships.

Summary

As we mentioned at the beginning of this chapter, the predictive propositions presented here represent only a few statements about basic social relationships. They provide no basic laws about human communicative behavior. They do, however, allow us to make some preliminary predictions and provide some direction for future scientific investigation. We can tentatively conclude that meeting people on a person-to-person basis seems characteristic of effective interpersonal relationships. Accurate empathy, a warm, positive, accepting attitude, and an open and supportive climate also describe effective relationships. Finally, effective interpersonal relationships occur when trust and a mutual acceptance of responsibility flourish.

We are not at all certain, however, which specific communicative behaviors reveal each of these attitudes, nor are we sure whether certain kinds of relations—such as husband–wife, manager–employee, pastor–communicant, teacher–student—demand different balances among these characteristics. Trust may be so overwhelmingly significant in some relationships that all else withers when trust is violated. We are still consumed with curiosity when an otherwise hostile and unaccepting man seems to establish an agreeable relationship with a lovely woman. Equally puzzling is the question of why many people are unable to establish better relationships. If the few things we know have some ring of truth, why is it that they seem to be disregarded so often? Maybe we need to know more. Therein lies the challenge.

Background Readings

The dynamics of interpersonal relationships focus on the fundamentals of person-to-person communication. These books outline a variety of different approaches to relationships and each one says something significant about the theory of people-in-relation-to-people.

Bennis, Warren G., Edgar H. Schein, Fred I. Steele, and David E. Berlew, *Interpersonal Dynamics: Essays and Readings on Human Interaction,* Rev. ed. (Homewood, Ill.: The Dorsey Press, 1968). Although the readings are provocative and substantial, the introductory essays summarize theoretical formulations concerning interpersonal relations and bring scientific knowledge to bear on issues of interpersonal relationships.

Combs, Arthur W., Donald L. Avila, and William W. Purkey, *Helping Relationships: Basic Concepts for the Helping Professions* (Boston: Allyn and Bacon, 1971). Although this book is written for people entering what is called "helping" professions, it explores the general question "What ideas about human behavior have special value for understanding and bringing about better relationships among people?" The book is devoted to basic principles but is written in an easy and readable style.

Luft, Joseph, *Of Human Interaction* (Palo Alto, Calif.: The National Press, 1969). This book is an explanation of the graphic model of interpersonal behavior called the "Johari Window," created by Luft and a colleague named Harry Ingham. The model is based on the assumption that awareness of behavior is an important concern in interpersonal interaction.

The model contains four "windows" representing open, blind, hidden, and unknown degrees of awareness of behavior, feelings, and motivation.

Rogers, Carl R., *On Becoming a Person* (Boston: Houghton Mifflin Co., 1961). This book has the subtitle of "A Therapist's View of Psychotherapy" and explores topics relevant to establishing helpful interpersonal relationships, especially when dealing with breakdowns in communication—interpersonal and intergroup.

Schutz, William C., *The Interpersonal Underworld* (Palo Alto, Calif.: Science & Behavior Books, 1966). This book is a reprint of Schutz's early publication called *FIRO: A Three-Dimensional Theory of Interpersonal Behavior.* FIRO stands for "Fundamental Interpersonal Relations Orientation." The entire approach is based on the assumption that interpersonal behavior stems from three needs: inclusion, control, and affection.

2.1 Interpersonal relationships tend to improve and communicative interaction increases when feelings are communicated directly and in a warm, expressive manner.

2.2 Interpersonal relationships tend to improve when both parties communicate what is happening in their private world through self-disclosure.

2.3 Interpersonal relationships tend to improve when both the parties communicate a warm, positive understanding of each other by giving relevant responses.

2.4 Interpersonal relationships tend to improve when both parties communicate a genuineness toward each other by expressing acceptance both verbally and nonverbally.

2.5 Interpersonal relationships tend to improve when both parties communicate an ongoing and unconditional positive regard for each other through nonevaluative, yet friendly, responses.

2.6 Interpersonal relationships tend to improve through constructive confrontation.

Chapter 2
Improving Relationships

In the preceding chapter we discussed some of the factors involved in interpersonal dynamics and effective interpersonal relationships. Let us now look at some more specific ways by which these relationships can be improved. Understanding the conditions important to establishing and maintaining desirable relationships is of little use, however, unless we also become aware of the specific methods and techniques contributing to these conditions. Effective relationships with others rarely happen by accident. Rather, the behaviors leading to them seem to be learned.

When we are skilled in helping others, our relationships with them usually improve with more speed, more satisfaction, and more certainty. We can focus our behavior along more profitable channels when we are able to identify desirable ways of acting and responding to others. The propositions in this chapter are concerned directly with the methods by which people communicate feelings, express helpful listening styles, provide responses of accurate understanding, and reveal warmth, liking, and trust. As we study the propositions, we may discover how particular methods of communicating help to produce better interpersonal relationships.

Predictive Propositions

2.1 Interpersonal relationships tend to improve and communicative interaction increases when feelings are communicated directly and in a warm, expressive manner.

The manner in which we choose to express our feelings to others is an important factor in interpersonal communication. When our feelings do not come across clearly, effective relationships are injured. One reason for this kind of failure is that such expression of feelings may take many different forms. For example, we may express our feelings through physiological changes, such as an increased heartbeat, deeper breathing, trembling, or blushing. We may also express them by the way in which we behave: we may either hug or hit someone, or just smile. Perhaps, we may express them by giving directives like "Shut up"; or by labeling people by saying "You are rude"; or by making statements of approval or disapproval, such as "You are wonderful" or "You are rotten." Not only is it possible to express the same feelings in many different ways, but it is also possible to express different feelings in the same ways. For example, a blush may indicate a person feels flattered, or embarrassed, or even angry. In other words, a nonverbal indication of feelings may be interpreted inaccurately and, perhaps, even mislead the other person.

This proposition suggests that relationships can be improved when feelings are expressed directly and with warmth. In other words, we should help others to understand by describing how we feel in terms that refer directly to the feelings we are experiencing. For example, rather than saying "You are wonderful," we could describe our feelings by saying "When you behave in that manner, you make me feel good and warm all over." Of course, the clearest message occurs when the description of what we are feeling matches and reinforces what is being expressed by our actions and is communicated with warmth. The objective of talking about feelings directly is to begin dialogs that will help to improve relationships with other persons. After all, if we expect others to take our feelings into account, we need to make sure they know how we feel. Research indicates that direct expressions of feelings can have a positive effect on others' behavior and can increase the amount of communicative interaction occurring, especially when the feelings and their expression are warm and direct.

Abstract

Michael M. Reece and Robert M. Whitman, "Expressive Movements, Warmth, and Verbal Reinforcement," *Journal of Abnormal and Social Psychology,* Vol. 64 (1962), pp. 234–236.

In this study Reece and Whitman were attempting to discover whether warmth has a reinforcing influence upon verbal behavior as measured by the total number of words expressed. In addition, they were concerned with whether warmth combined with verbal reinforcement would produce a greater total reinforcing effect upon verbalization.

Each subject was asked to say—in responses recorded on tape—whatever words came to mind during a 15-minute preassociation period. Subjects in the study were assigned to four groups: (1) warm–reinforced, (2) warm–nonreinforced, (3) cold–reinforced, (4) cold–nonreinforced. The experimenter created the warm condition by leaning toward the subject and, smiling, looking directly at the subject while keeping his hands still. The cold condition was created by the experimenter leaning away from the subject and without smiling, drumming his fingers while looking everywhere but at the subject. He verbally reinforced plural nouns by saying "Mm–hmmm." Except for giving the instructions, he verbalized nothing else. At the end of the experiment, tapes were replayed and both the frequency of all verbal responses and of the plural nouns, which had been verbally reinforced, were tabulated.

This study shows that the total number of words was significantly affected by the expressive movements and the verbal reinforcement. However, verbal reinforcement alone did not seem to be a significant influence. In other words, it took the direct expression of warmth combined with the verbal reinforcement to achieve the positive results.

■ The study also implies that the direct expression of feelings, particularly the feeling of warmth, increases the amount of verbal communicative behavior between individuals. The expression of feelings through both what is said and what is done can have an effect on what other people do and say. As feelings are communicated, individuals tend to be that much closer to one another.

2.2 Interpersonal relationships tend to improve when both parties communicate what is happening in their private world through self-disclosure.

Self-disclosure refers to the process of revealing to others how we are reacting, primarily inside, to what is happening now. It also occurs when we give information about how we have reacted in the past as a means of helping others to understand our present reactions. Assuming that a person comes to understand us by knowing how we react to things, self-disclosure can have a direct influence on our relationships with others. It is particularly effective in improving relationships when it deals with reactions occurring in the present with respect to people and happenings at any given moment. Research on self-disclosure seems to indicate the more we reveal about ourselves to a person, the greater the likelihood of his or her liking us. An interesting corollary is that we are more likely to self-disclose to someone we know fairly well and like than to someone we do not know or do not like. Self-disclosure requires that we take the risk of being rejected. This may explain why some research suggests that a person who engages in self-disclosure tends to view his or her fellow human beings as basically good rather than basically evil people.

Abstract

Sidney M. Jourard, "Self-Disclosure and Other Effective Cathexis," *Journal of Abnormal and Social Psychology,* Vol. 59 (1959), pp. 428–433.

Jourard tried to determine whether the amount of personal information a person has disclosed to others and the information he knows about others has any direct relationship to the emotional attachment he has for others. To determine this, he administered a self-disclosure questionnaire of 15 items to faculty members in a nurses' college. These subjects were asked to disclose the answers to questions about themselves to the researcher and then indicate to which of their colleagues they had disclosed each item. Subjects were then asked to indicate which items of information each colleague had told them. Finally, they rank-ordered the other subjects in terms of liking.

The subjects tended to disclose more information to those colleagues whom they ranked as liking more. They also tended to know more about these same colleagues, indicating a shared relationship.

■ Other studies support Jourard's findings, which also strongly suggest that such a shared relationship between two people tends to make both more supportive and accepting, thus strengthening the bond. As we develop a more effective interpersonal relationship with others, we will tend to have fewer secrets and fewer blind spots in our behavior. We will learn more about ourselves and be more aware of and understanding of others. Developing a willingness to be self-disclosing and an ability to support and accept others when they are self-disclosing is important in improving interpersonal relationships.

2.3 Interpersonal relationships tend to improve when both the parties communicate a warm, positive understanding of each other by giving relevant responses.

As we use the term here, a "relevant" response refers to any verbal or nonverbal means of showing or demonstrating to the other person what his or her statement, idea, or comment means to us. Most of us have a very strong tendency to react to someone else's comment before we really understand what the other person means. We are so involved with what we want to say that we make no effort to understand the other person as he or she would like, and we fail to demonstrate what we do understand so that the other person can then correct us. In developing close friendly interpersonal relationships, it is important to indicate to the other person that we clearly heard and understood what he or she intended. Often in interpersonal relationships we will find that one or both individuals involved have not clearly heard or accurately understood the other. Relevant responses demand that we indicate that we care about what the other person is saying and are trying to understand what he or she means. One very effective way of providing relevant responses is to restate the other person's ideas in our own words, attempting to reveal the meaning we have assigned them. Such responses provide us with a method that tests the accuracy of our understanding while at the same time expressing a warm, supportive attitude.

Abstract

David W. Johnson, "Effects of Warmth of Interaction, Accuracy of Understanding, and the Proposal of Compromises on Listener's Behavior," *Journal of Counseling Psychology*, Vol. 18 (1971), pp. 207–216.

Johnson's concern was with whether or not a relevant response that accurately expresses understanding of the other person's position leads to a feeling of being clearly heard and understood, thus reducing defensive adherence to one's position and feelings of being threatened and thereby resulting in a willingness to reach an agreement in a negotiation.

The research designed for this study required that confederates be trained to negotiate and reverse roles in ways that (1) expressed warmness or coldness, (2) gave complete and accurate or incomplete and inaccurate restatements of the other's position and feelings, and (3) proposed either a series of compromises or none at all. The individuals involved in the study were placed in groups of four, consisting of two subjects and two confederates. The subjects were told they were competing against another group of four in a different room. Each group was given a description of a hypothetical court case dealing with a civil law suit. While one group was asked to develop a defense for the club being sued, the other group supported the party doing the suing. At a 15-minute meeting devoted to arriving at a joint solution, a representative from each group had five minutes to present his or her group's position to another group's representative. Members of each group were to be paid varying amounts depending on when a joint agreement was reached and how close it was to each group's original position. Negotiations took place in pairs, consisting of one subject and one confederate.

In this study relationships were found between the expressed accuracy of understanding, the act of proposing compromises, and the degree of cooperation in a negotiation. Relationships were also found between expressed warmth and the degree of favorable interpersonal attitudes. More agreements were reached when accurate understanding responses were given. The subjects made a greater effort to understand confederates and also viewed them as being more understanding when relevant responses were communicated. In addition, more agreements were reached in less time when the confederates proposed compromises.

■ It is reasonably clear that if a person wishes to influence another, responses that indicate accuracy of understanding are probably important. In addition, if a person wishes to develop a positive relationship with another, expressions of warmth are probably crucial. Relevant responses indicate an accurate understanding and encourage cooperation between parties, making the expression of warmth and more favorable interpersonal attitudes possible. An interesting sidelight to this study is that the confederates were able to learn to give responses of both warmth and accurate understanding. This may hopefully mean that such responses can be learned, that we may be able to improve our ability to give relevant responses. Such responses do seem to be conducive to improving interpersonal relationships.

2.4 Interpersonal relationships tend to improve when both parties communicate a genuineness toward each other by expressing acceptance both verbally and nonverbally.

The communication of acceptance on the part of both parties involved in a relationship seems to be vital to developing and maintaining mutual satisfaction. This mutual expression of acceptance leads not only to feelings of security and psychological safety but also to a generalized feeling of being supported. Developing satisfying, close kinds of relationships demands that we be able to communicate acceptance of others. Such acceptance is communicated most strongly through verbal and nonverbal expressions of warmth and liking and through showing an honest desire to understand the other person by taking his ideas and feelings seriously.

Abstract

Benjamin Pope and Aron Walfe Siegman,
"Interviewer Warmth," in *Studies in Dyadic
Communication*, eds. A. W. Siegman and
B. Pope (New York: Pergamon Press, 1972),
pp. 73–80.

This study attempted to discover whether or not interviewers who express warmth tend to elicit higher productivity, less resistance, less hesitation, and greater fluency than those interviewers who do not express warmth. To answer this question, Siegman and Pope developed a study that began by arousing warm or cold expectancies for interviewer behavior prior to the time interviews took place. During the interviews themselves, the actual behavior was varied according to the aroused expectancies. Each subject had one warm and one cold interview. Warm interviewer behavior involved smiling, head nodding, and speaking warmly. Cold interviewer behavior involved not smiling, no head nods, and drab and cold vocal expressions. Subject resistance, productivity (number of words produced per response), hesitation, and fluency were measured and percentage scores calculated by using the number of responses in each category (words per minute, etc.) as the numerator and the total number of responses as the denominator.

The subjects' perceptions were consistent with the behaviors the interviewers expressed. Subjects perceived the warm interviewers as being significantly warmer, more accepting, more understanding, more pleasant, more responsive, more friendly, and more interested than those showing cold behavior. Subjects also liked the warm interviewers better, felt they were better liked by them, and were consistently happier at the prospect of these interviewers' becoming their therapists. The subjects also uttered significantly more words per response in the warm situations than in the cold. Interestingly, when the subjects experienced the warm interview first and then the cold interview, there was a strong carryover effect from the warm to the cold situation. It was more difficult, on the other hand, to create a positive interpersonal relationship when the cold interview occurred first.

■ Much of the research on this proposition indicates that acceptance is communicated more often than not through verbal and nonverbal expressions of warmth. The study also seems to support the idea that warmth is necessary for personal and interpersonal growth. Out of warmth and acceptance we develop a climate that produces a supporting, stimulating, and satisfying relationship.

2.5 Interpersonal relationships tend to improve when both parties communicate an ongoing and unconditional positive regard for each other through nonevaluative, yet friendly, responses.

Many of our problems in interpersonal relationships result from our strong tendency to evaluate—to make judgments about—people, things, and events. Evaluative statements are those that state, suggest, or imply approval or disapproval. They include such statements as "You are strong," "You are right," or "You are stupid." Nonevaluative responses consist of reactions that express supportiveness, understanding, and respect. Giving nonevaluative responses does not mean that we should avoid indicating to another how we feel about something, even the other person's behavior. It does mean that we should describe our feelings directly and avoid sarcasm, giving commands, name calling, or making accusations and other kinds of statements that involve evaluating or judging the other person.

Such comments often are designed to create, and even more often result in hostility and the destruction of effective relationships between individuals.

Abstract

Kenneth Heller, John B. Davis, and Roger A. Myers, "The Effects of Interviewer Style in a Standard Interview," *Journal of Consulting Psychology,* Vol. 30 (1966), pp. 501-508.

In this study, Heller, David, and Myers were attempting to discover the effects of friendly, hostile, and neutral communicator styles on the interviewer's length of response, type of response, and feelings during response. Actors were trained to exhibit active and friendly, active and hostile, passive and friendly, and passive and hostile interviewer styles. After subjects listened to a taped narrative of a college student discussing his or her problems, they each talked to an interviewer for 15 minutes. For the first five minutes of the interview, they were asked to remember and report as much about the taped explanation as they could. For the next five minutes, they discussed how they might solve situations presented on the tapes. For the last five minutes, they were asked to give their honest evaluation of the counseling period. During the interviews, the trained interviewers consistently responded in active–friendly or active–hostile and passive–friendly or passive–hostile styles. At the conclusion of each interview, each subject completed an inventory stating his or her reaction to the interview, his or her performance in it, and his or her reaction to the interviewer. The amount of time each subject spent talking during the 15-minute period was computed and a content analysis of subject responses was made.

As our proposition suggests, hostile interviewers were liked the least, and friendly interviewers were liked the best. Active interviewers were most successful in sustaining the verbalization rates of their subjects. Subjects exposed to active–friendly interviewers used the greatest proportion of family words. Silence was more inhibiting than either hostile or friendly styles.

■ The study also shows that hostile behavior, characterized most often by evaluative statements designed to demean others, does not improve interpersonal relationships but causes deterioration in them. Interpersonal relationships are improved most often when the parties involved express friendly, nonevaluative statements that provide support and reduce defensiveness. Such nonevaluative, friendly reinforcement is vitally important in improving sagging relationships since they communicate trust, acceptance, and genuineness. They provide us with the means of letting the other person know that we regard him or her in a positive way, thus providing an effective means of improving interpersonal relationships.

2.6 Interpersonal relationships tend to improve through constructive confrontation.

Confrontation, in this context, refers to the act of explaining to another person as nonevaluatively, accurately, and honestly as we can why we find it impossible or even difficult to agree with him. It represents an invitation to someone else to reconsider or to reflect upon his behavior. Although usually it involves direct inter-action between two individuals, it is possible with modern technology—such as a video recorder—to provide a sort of self-confrontation. Constructive confrontation is an act of communication designed to encourage self-examination. It is not an act of punishment, even though it may seem difficult to engage in confrontation without being punitive; however, developing the ability to engage in constructive confrontation is part of improving interpersonal relationships. It is the rare individual who is able to confront himself, become aware of his own behaviors, and then be committed to changing them. Most of us are unable to make these changes on our own. We need friends who will take the time and effort to provide constructive and supportive criticism that can be used to stimulate personal growth.

Abstract

Harry S. Boyd and Vernon D. Sisney, "Immediate Self-Image Confrontation and Changes in Self-Concept," *Journal of Consulting Psychology,* Vol. 31 (1967), pp. 291–294.

Boyd and Sisney were concerned with the use of confrontation as a means of improving one's self-concept. In this study they were particularly interested in whether confrontation with a video-tape recording of one's own behavior can create a shift from a less to a more accurate self-image.

Fourteen subjects were selected from male in-patients of a neuropsychiatric ward in a veterans' hospital and randomly assigned to experimental and control groups similar in both average age and diagnostic condition. Several days before the experiment began, subjects were administered the Leary Interpersonal Check List, which allows each subject to describe his self-concept with an adjective checklist containing descriptions of various kinds of interpersonal attitudes and behavior. For the experiment, each subject was individually brought into a room containing an unconcealed video camera and recording equipment, then asked to participate in a 10-minute standardized interview. The interview covered each individual's reactions and feelings concerning the other subjects, himself, his family, the experiment in progress, and the experimenters. Following the interview, all subjects were instructed to watch the monitor near them. The interview was immediately replayed for the experimental group while the control group was shown a segment of a daytime television comedy. After giving each subject an opportunity to ask questions or talk about how he felt, he was cautioned not to talk about the experiment with other patients. The Leary Interpersonal Check List was then given in a different room for the second time. Two weeks later each subject was given the Leary Interpersonal Check List for the third time.

In the experimental group the self-concept scores of subjects—those allowed to view the video tape of their interview—obtained after the video tape confrontation tended to be less distorted and more accurate immediately after the confrontation and persisted over the two-week period. The experimental subject's public self-concept and own self-concept also moved closer together. These results strongly support the usefulness of self-image confrontation in producing measurable and positive effect on a person's self-concept.

■ Constructive confrontation appears to be a means by which desirable changes can be brought about in people. The process of learning more about one's self through the comments and descriptions of others or through the facilities of video-taped recordings appears to be helpful in developing an accurate self-concept, which in turn leads to a climate in which people can talk openly and supportively. When it is used in constructive ways, confrontation can facilitate the improvement of interpersonal relationships.

Summary

Effective relationships with other people do not happen by accident. The behaviors involved in improving these relationships seem to be learned. Interpersonal relationships can be improved by communicating feelings directly, through self-disclosure, through relevant responses demonstrating positive understanding, and through warm and friendly feelings. They are also improved by expressing acceptance both verbally and nonverbally, by showing unconditional positive regard for others through nonevaluative responses, and by engaging in constructive confrontation. Relationships improve more speedily, with more satisfaction, and with more certainty as we become more skilled in the methods and techniques of helping others.

Background Readings

Methods of bringing about better relationships with others appear as suggestions in the popular literature and in a series of current publications having to do with communication in interpersonal relations. These books include some theory but seek to integrate suggestions for more effective practice of interpersonal communication.

Brown, Charles T., and Charles Van Riper, *Communication in Human Relationships* (Skokie, Ill.: National Textbook Co., 1973). This book begins with and develops from the premise that people are in a state of alienation. Later chapters explain how interpersonal communication can help people to cope with alienation and establish meaningful relationships with one another.

Giffin, Kim, and Bobby R. Patton, *Fundamentals of Interpersonal Communication* (New York: Harper & Row, 1971). Much of the material in this book is designed to provide information that will help the reader acquire new insights about himself and his or her relationships with others. Suggested applications, learning experiences, and guidelines help the reader to make changes in behavior.

Johnson, David W., *Reaching Out: Interpersonal Effectiveness and Self-Actualization* (Englewood Cliffs, N. J.: Prentice-Hall, 1972). This book provides small doses of theory and large numbers of experiences for developing effective interpersonal skills.

Keltner, John W., *Interpersonal Speech-Communication: Elements and Structures* (Belmont, Calif.: Wadsworth Publishing Co., 1970). This book is designed to help the reader to develop his or her own communication skills in order to change and improve conditions in his or her own life and in society. A "try this" section at the end of each chapter includes suggestions to help in developing applications.

Pace, R. Wayne, and Robert R. Boren, *The Human Transaction: Facets, Functions, and Forms of Interpersonal Communication* (Glenview, Ill.: Scott, Foresman and Co., 1973). This book contains theory and specific methods for improving interpersonal relationships. It includes a helpful section on language, with a part on language practices that can facilitate communicative accuracy.

Pace, R. Wayne, Brent D. Peterson, and Terrence R. Radcliffe, *Communicating Interpersonally: A Reader* (Columbus, Ohio: Charles E. Merrill Publishing Co., 1973). This collection of readings has a section on amelioration of interpersonal communication that includes articles on improving listening and developing effective interpersonal communication.

Peterson, Brent D., Gerald M. Goldhaber, and R. Wayne Pace, *Communication Probes* (Palo Alto, Calif.: Science Research Associates, 1974). A text-reader that presents principles and methods of interpersonal communication in an easy, entertaining format. Through the use of cartoons, music, poetry, advertisements, and short essays, this book reveals ideas about how to be effective communicators.

Part 2
Messages

Person-to-person communication involves one individual serving as the primary source of an idea and another serving as the perceiver and interpreter of what the first person says and does. After initiating interaction, communicators soon discover that the ideas they wish to share with others cannot be physically, surgically, or magically inserted into people's minds. Only through messages is anyone intentionally able to initiate the procedures by which ideas can be shared. The only connection that exists between a source and an interpreter is a message.

Messages may consist of sound waves produced by the human vocal system, marks produced by writing or printing, diagrams and pictures produced by an artist, an arrangement of office furniture, letters produced by a computer, or even silence or any other stimuli that someone can receive through his or her senses and interpret. As long as an individual can assign meaning to the behavior of other people, to objects, to events, the potential for a message exists. In other words, anything that an individual does might well be a message, provided another person can assign meaning to it.

The interpretations or meanings that individuals create can be determined in part by the arrangement of a message's elements. If you deliberately structure sounds or sights in a particular pattern, the likelihood increases that an observer or a listener will interpret the message closer to what you had in mind than if you made no effort to create a meaningful pattern. However, regardless of whether or not we make an effort to encourage a specific interpretation of a message, *some* pattern will always exist and have the potential of being interpreted. That is, we cannot *not* communicate. The task is to determine *what* messages will be interpreted and *how* they will be interpreted. All messages have potentially at least two meanings: the one *intended* by the person sending the message and the one *created* by the person receiving the message. In understanding another person, the meaning that really counts is the one created by the receiver of the message. Regardless of what we might have intended, the receiver can and often does misinterpret. His interpretation is what makes a difference.

The way in which a person interprets, misinterprets, understands, and creates meaning out of the message he or she receives is what we call *message reception* and *processing*. However, reception and processing imply more than what actually takes place, since the receiver of a message creates meaning based on his or her prior experience and the stimuli constituting the message. Rather than message reception, we might more accurately say *meaning creation*; instead of message processing, we might more accurately say *meaning transformation*. However, the terms "message reception" and "processing" represent a useful semantic compromise: we can build on former experiences with these concepts and gradually make the transition to thinking and talking about communicative behavior in a more scientific manner.

The manner in which a person selects, arranges, embellishes, displays, and otherwise makes the message clear, interesting, and appealing is called *message preparation and presentation*. In this case, the preparation and presentation of a message is a literal, or real, task; that is, elements of oral and written language are structured, diagrams are created and colored, furniture is arranged, and so on. As important as the ways in which messages are designed are the ways in which they are presented. Vocal expression, pictorial display, combinations of audio and visual media, and the use of special individuals and locations for the most favorable exposure are aspects of presentation that may influence how the message is interpreted. In the chapters of this section, we shall examine the data indicating *what* factors influence message reception, processing, preparation, and presentation and *how* they do it.

3.1 Oral message reception is enhanced when the person talking speaks between 125 and 190 words per minute.

3.2 Oral message reception is enhanced when a listener has intelligence, scholastic aptitude, and a good vocabulary.

3.3 Oral message reception is enhanced when the listener is motivated to obtain information.

3.4 Oral message reception is enhanced when nonverbal messages, such as gestures and visual aids, are received simultaneously with verbal messages.

3.5 Oral message reception is enhanced when major ideas are strengthened through reinforcement.

3.6 Oral messages tend to be selectively received and processed so they are consistent with the listener's perceptions and background.

3.7 Oral messages that we receive and process but that are inconsistent with our attitudes tend to create cognitive dissonance within us.

Chapter 3
Message Reception and Processing

Recently a young college professor, deep in thought over a research paper he was preparing for a professional convention, entered his home after work to find his wife excited about a special men's tie sale at a local department store. "Honey, we must go to this sale," she said. "The ties are only $1.99 and I can't even buy the material to make a tie for that price." "Ok," replied the young professor as he entered his study. After thinking about his research paper and the convention for a while, he picked up the sports page of the evening paper and noticed an ad next to the ball scores that read as follows: *Tie Sale —Exclusive Tie Sale —One Time Only —$4.99 Ties on Sale for $1.99!! One Day Only!!* He immediately hurried to his wife in the kitchen and exclaimed, "Dear, guess what I just read in the paper? Ties are on sale for $1.99 today. Let's hurry with supper so we can go downtown and buy a supply." Needless to say, his wife quickly let him know that he never listened to her.

This chapter will deal with the way in which we receive and process messages. In it we will discuss propositions that concern the optimum conditions under which a listener can best receive and understand oral messages. Hopefully, we will find methods of avoiding the typical poor listening situations illustrated by the young professor and his wife.

Predictive Propositions

3.1 Oral message reception is enhanced when the person talking speaks between 125 and 190 words per minute.

In the mid-1920s W. Norwood Brigance (1926), after studying the winners in intercollegiate oratorical contests, determined that the winners spoke at approximately 120 words per minute. Since then, many speech teachers, educators, and communication researchers have studied speaking rates to determine the optimum rate at which listeners can comprehend messages effectively. Generally, this research suggests that a variety of rates between 125 and 190 words per minute are effective in enhancing message reception (Thompson, 1967, pp. 88–90). Additional research has indicated that we have the cognitive ability to receive and comprehend messages at much faster rates (Nichols and Stevens, 1957). If this is accurate, it means that we have time for distractions and letting our minds wander while we listen at lower rates. However, we can also use this time to focus on other aspects of the message besides the words being spoken. The research on rate of speaking has covered a large variety of speakers and situations and has used widely varied data-collection techniques. However, for the most part, it seems strongly to favor our proposition that listeners receive messages and comprehend them best at rates between 125 and 190 words per minute.

Abstract

Kenneth A. Harwood, "Listenability and Rate of Presentation," *Speech Monographs*, Vol. 22 (March 1955), pp. 57–59.

Harwood was interested in determining whether or not listenability was affected significantly by rate of presentation. In addition, the study also attempted to determine whether readability was a consistent predictor of listenability at the different rates.

For the study, a series of seven stories was constructed so that (1) the predicted readability of one of the stories fell at the midpoint of one of each of seven successive ranges of reading ease described by Flesch and that (2) the predicted human interest value of each story fell at the midpoint of the middle range of human interest he describes. Each story, recorded by the same male voice, was 300 words long and taped at the separate rates of 125, 150, 175, and 200 words per minute. The subjects used were 487 tenth-grade students who were split into four groups of similar sex, age, IQ, and reading comprehension.

In general, listenability decreased with an increase in the rate of presentation. However, the mean listenability at each rate of presentation did not differ significantly. The story whose readability was predicted to be fairly difficult was found to be significantly less listenable when it was presented at the rate of 200 words per minute than when it was presented at 175 words per minute. The listenability of the stories at each rate of presentation was highly consistent with their predicted readability. In fact, within the limits and under the conditions studied here, readability might be used as the gross predictor of listenability.

■ Importantly, the rate of speaking does have a potential effect upon our ability to communicate with others. As this research indicates, we should be careful not to speak so rapidly that the listenability of what we say decreases. It is probably just as important to be aware of the limitations of lower rates. When we speak more slowly than 125 words per minute, it becomes more difficult for our listeners to concentrate on what we are saying because they have too much time to let their minds wander. Generally speaking, a rate between 125 and 190 words per minute will be the most effective in helping our listeners gain the most from what we have to say.

3.2 Oral message reception is enhanced when a listener has intelligence, scholastic aptitude, and a good vocabulary.

A considerable amount of research has attempted to analyze the relationship between listening and factors such as intelligence, scholastic aptitude, and vocabulary. Many listening researchers contend that present listening tests are largely measures of these three factors. As we consider this predictive proposition, we should keep this possibility in mind. It may well be that the research indicating the relationship between listening and these three factors does so because of the invalidity of existing listening tests.

For the most part, persons who score well on standardized IQ tests will probably also score well on standardized listening tests (Thompson, 1967, pp. 133–136). In addition, there appears to be a moderate-to-high relationship between listening and scholastic aptitude. However, results of research dealing with the relationship between size of vocabulary and listening comprehension have been conflicting. Yet, generally, the research seems to indicate that a relationship does exist between the ability to comprehend information and the size of one's vocabulary. Efforts to improve vocabulary are also likely to improve listening acuity.

Abstract

Bernice P. Biggs, "Construction, Validation, and Evaluation of a Diagnostic Test of Listening Effectiveness," *Speech Monographs,* Vol. 23 (March 1956), pp. 9–13.

This study attempted both to develop a test that would measure several aspects of listening behavior and to validate this test against outside criteria. Biggs constructed seven tests to constitute the diagnostic battery. The measure used for validating the battery was an instructor-rating scale that called for checking one of three behavior descriptions.

■ The study seems to indicate that it is possible to develop a statistically valid and reliable diagnostic listening test and that the listening behavior sampled by the various subtests of the diagnostic battery describes some portion of the listening process. In relationship to our particular predictive proposition, the study's results may indicate that the relationship between intelligence, scholastic aptitude, and vocabulary has more foundation than simply the invalidity of existing tests. This seems even more apparent when we recognize that the correlation between the scores on the listening test used in this study and the scores on the American Council on Education Psychological tests for college freshmen was quite high, indicating that scholastic aptitude is probably an important factor in how well a person does on a listening test.

Obviously, much additional research work will have to be done to solve the dispute about the relationship between listening and these three factors. However, it does seem apparent that if one has intelligence, high scholastic aptitude, and a good vocabulary, he has the potential of being a good oral message receiver, along with having many of the basic qualities necessary for becoming a good listener. At the same time, such abilities do not guarantee effective listening behavior, which involves some conscious effort on the part of the receiver as well.

3.3 Oral message reception is enhanced when the listener is motivated to obtain information.

This may be one of our propositions that simply supports what we suspect from common sense. Most of us believe that if we really care about a message, we tend to concentrate on it to such a degree that we become more effective listeners. For example, if your boyfriend were to ask you for a date to go to a concert of your favorite rock group, you would probably listen quite intently. But even though the relationship between reception and motivation seems obvious, a great deal of effort has been made to establish it scientifically. As one might suspect, however, the research has generally indicated that a relationship does exist between the two.

Abstract

Daniel W. Mullin, "An Experimental Study of Retention in Educational Television," *Speech Monographs*, Vol. 24 (March 1957), pp. 31–38.

Mullin was interested in determining whether or not motivation would be effective in increasing the viewer's retention of educational television, both in the home and the classroom. Would there also be differences in retention in these two situations? To find answers to these questions, he had a 23-minute educational television program produced with as much expertise as experimental conditions allowed. Subjects included high school juniors of both sexes, with and without the motivation to learn, from three different schools in the same city. Some of the boys and girls viewed the television program in their home while others viewed it in the classroom.

Regardless of the location in which the viewing took place, the learning score of the motivated viewer was significantly higher than that of the unmotivated viewer. In other words, motivation was significantly effective in increasing retention scores of both the home viewer and the classroom viewer.

■ It seems apparent, then, that motivation is an important factor in effective listening. In other words, if we wish to become more effective in our listening behavior and retain the maximum information from a situation, we must learn to be more motivated about the topic being considered. These same implications also apply to the source of messages. If we are sending the message and wish to maximize our effectiveness, we must create circumstances that will increase the motivation of those listening to us, so they will want to retain the information we are disseminating.

3.4 Oral message reception is enhanced when nonverbal messages, such as gestures and visual aids, are received simultaneously with verbal messages.

Nonverbal messages include those messages we communicate to others by our delivery, dress, mood, gestures, facial expressions, and the situation in which we are communicating. Accurate reception of these nonverbal messages requires considering them in conjunction with the verbal messages and interpreting them simultaneously. For example, research with facial expressions indicates that without verbal cues meaning conveyed by the face is difficult to understand. On the other hand, these same facial expressions strongly reinforce and increase the accuracy of our interpretation of verbal messages. In other words, nonverbal stimuli are important for reinforcing verbal messages, and both verbal and nonverbal messages must be received for a listener to predict accurately the meaning of the nonverbal messages.

Evidence indicates that a listener tends to understand and retain more information if the speaker can be seen as well as heard. With the listener present, the speaker can use both auditory and visual means for conveying information. In the early 1930s, Ewbank (1932) compared the relative effectiveness of a live-audience speech and one given on the radio. They discovered that not only did listeners gain more information from the live speech but they also preferred it to the radio lecture. Subjects indicated that they "like to see the person who is speaking." Such results help explain the appeal of television, where viewers have the advantage of seeing speakers in clearer detail than they can, on occasion, in person.

Abstract

John Holway Ulrich, "An Experimental Study of the Acquisition of Information from Three Types of Recorded Television Presentations," *Speech Monographs,* Vol. 24 (March 1957), pp. 39–45.

This study was an attempt to determine whether or not subjects would retain more information from observing a television recording of a lecture without visual aids, from one with visual aids handled by the instructor, or from one where the visual aids were simply flashed on the television screen. The subjects from 40 eighth-grade classes in Chicago, saw a lecture dealing with food resources of Africa and took a quiz developed to measure their retention. Poster-type visual aids were planned for each unit of information in the lecture, which was given in all three treatment groups, and a visual aid was constructed to correspond to each test item.

As this predictive proposition would lead us to believe, the subjects in this study immediately recalled more information from a television recording of the lecture supported by poster-type visual aids than from the one without aids. Interestingly, whether the lecturer handled the visual aids or simply flashed them on the television screen at the appropriate moment seemed to have little effect on the recall of information. Another interesting finding was that, after a period of 30 days, the differences in comprehension between the lecture employing visual aids and those without them tended to disappear.

■ Bringing together the nonverbal messages and verbal messages provides a means of enhancing our efforts to communicate with others. Certainly, the use of nonverbal means, including visual aids, can increase the degree of comprehension and recall. If we desire to maximize our ability to communicate with other people, we must bring together both the verbal and the nonverbal dimensions of the messages we send. Such a combination will enhance our opportunities to help others understand what we are saying.

3.5 Oral message reception is enhanced when major ideas are strengthened through reinforcement.

Reinforcement deals with highlighting or emphasizing major points to create a greater likelihood of message reception and understanding. A variety of rhetorical devices can be used to emphasize major points, such as repetition, restatement, and illustration. Anything that serves to highlight, emphasize, or amplify an idea or point is a means of reinforcement. As we learned earlier, the major points in a speech are more easily remembered than details. However, we tend to remember these major ideas best when they are reinforced. Such reinforcement may take place through actively involving the audience in the communication situation because individuals who try to acquire information in situations in which perceptual and motor responses are demanded usually learn more effectively. For example, lectures (informative speeches designed to communicate information) in which the audience responds in writing, to themselves orally, or even to machines will be superior to passive listening situations for diffusing information. McKeachie (1963, p. 1132) reviewed dozens of studies on lecturing in educational settings and observed that "the lecture is an effective way of communicating information." He further suggested that even though lectures seem less organized than textbooks, films, and teaching machines, the ability of the lecturer to respond to the audience makes for greater effectiveness than a carefully organized, inflexible presentation.

Taking notes during a lecture can improve the reception and retention of information. The physical act of notetaking reinforces the ideas being presented. Crawford (1925) found a significant and positive correlation between the number of concepts and ideas recorded definitely, clearly, and fully in student notes taken during lectures and the ideas they were able to recall at the time of a quiz. Interestingly, no correlation was found between scores of students on intelligence tests and the kind of notes they took. Another method of reinforcement is the anticipation that the ideas presented may be useful later. Such anticipation appears to increase the individual's involvement with the message and thus encourages the retention of ideas. Jones and Aneshausel (1956) discovered that the anticipation of having to construct counterarguments resulted in significantly greater retention of the arguments presented in a persuasive message.

Abstract

C. E. Crawford, "Some Experimental Studies as a Result of College Note-Taking," *Journal of Educational Research,* Vol. 12 (Dec. 1925), pp. 379–386.

Crawford was directly concerned with discovering whether taking notes during a lecture would result in higher quiz scores than listening carefully without taking notes. To answer this question he conducted a series of seven experiments involving students enrolled in regular college courses. During the first experiment, Group A was instructed to take notes while Group B listened carefully without taking notes. Immediately following the lecture, an essay or true-false quiz was given. For the next experiment the procedure was reversed: Group A listening without taking notes and Group B taking notes. The essay and the true-false quizzes were given a day later and then again several weeks later. The experiment was repeated seven times.

Students who took notes scored higher on quizzes than those who listened passively. When the results were measured by an essay quiz immediately after a lecture, the note takers showed a high degree of superiority over the others. As measured by a similar quiz given days or weeks later, the note takers showed a marked superiority over the others. When the results were measured by a true-false test immediately after the lecture, the note takers showed a slight inferiority; however, when measured days or weeks later by a true-false test, the note takers again scored higher.

■ Studies in which subjects have been actively involved (taking notes, preparing for a debate, or anticipating some future use of the information during a lecture) demonstrate that such involvement helps in retaining information. Other methods of reinforcing ideas also help in this retention. If we wish to have our listeners receive our messages and remember them, we have a greater chance of success if we reinforce our message in some way, either through such rhetorical strategies as repetition and illustration or through getting the listener to reinforce the message for himself through active participation and anticipation.

3.6 Oral messages tend to be selectively received and processed so they are consistent with the listener's perceptions and background.

We constantly receive a variety of oral messages. In fact, so many messages bombard us that we must select the ones we will receive, attend to, and process. Many variables come into play in deciding which messages we will select and process. However, a major variable is the composite of our experiences and our behavior. Since none of us have had exactly similar experiences in our lives, this dissimilarity causes us to perceive reality in a different way from anyone else. The unique way people see the same reality may cause problems when they attempt to communicate. Four important tendencies related to background experiences and the way we select oral messages are *selective exposure, selective attention, selective perception,* and *selective retention.*

Selective Exposure   Reinforcement theories lead us to assume that we seek to reinforce our present attitudes, beliefs, values, and behaviors. Consistency theories suggest that we try to avoid a state of possible inconsistency when we receive messages incompatible with our prior or present behavior. Such avoidance of information is referred to as selective exposure. We select messages for processing that we assume will reinforce us and avoid those that conflict with our attitudes. Such selecting can occur unconsciously as well as consciously. As communicators, we must be aware of the background experiences and attitudes of those with whom we communicate so that we can present messages they will select as worthy of processing.

Selective Attention   People tend to avoid messages that are inconsistent or unrewarding. However, since it is impossible to avoid all messages, there is a strong tendency towards selective attention when we are exposed to unwanted messages. Those we tend to pay particular attention to are those that are consistent with our attitudes, beliefs, values, and behaviors.

Selective Perception   We can hardly hope to avoid exposure to all nonreinforcing or inconsistent messages. Even though most of us must pay attention to such messages at some time, this does not mean we will perceive them as being inconsistent or nonreinforcing. Through selective perception we may alter the meaning of the message in such a way that it becomes consistent with what we desire or expect to receive. Such selective perception may not be in accord with what others see as reality. For example, in a study by Arnold and McCroskey (1967), three messages about busing students to maintain racial balance were for test purposes variously attributed to Martin Luther King, Jr., or George C. Wallace. One was a strongly worded message in favor of busing, one was clearly opposed, and one was a moderate statement expressing both favorable and unfavorable views about busing. When the subjects read the moderate position, they perceived the message as strongly supportive of busing if it was attributed to King and strongly opposed if attributed to Wallace. Thus, through selective perception, we assign meanings that help us to avoid otherwise nonreinforcing or inconsistent messages.

Selective Retention   Even if a message survives the first three tendencies, there is no guarantee that we will receive and retain it. People seem to forget unrewarding or inconsistent messages and to remember those that are consistent and rewarding (Levine and Murphy, 1943). We may not even remember having been exposed to certain messages.

Abstract

Hans Sebald, "Limitations of Communication: Mechanisms of Image Maintenance in Form of Selective Perception, Selective Memory and Selective Distortion," *Journal of Communication*, Vol. 12 (1962), pp. 142–149.

Sebald was interested in exploring what would happen if an individual encountered a presentation where both his and an opposing point of view were aired. The problem of an individual's failing to expose himself to messages with which he does not agree was avoided. In the study 152 university students who had watched the 1960 Kennedy–Nixon presidential debates filled out questionnaires designed to assess their attitudes or changes of attitudes toward the two presidential candidates before and after the debates.

Sebald found that a form of selective exposure occurred since a subject tended to concentrate on those segments of the communication that supported his or her views. The viewer took from the Kennedy–Nixon debates information that preserved (1) a favorable image of the preferred party's candidate and (2) an unfavorable image of the opposing party's candidate. Subjects selected those materials consistent with their existing beliefs and also selectively perceived other material so that it would be consistent with these same beliefs.

■ Messages that are consistent with our attitudes, beliefs, values, and behaviors, or at least appear to be reinforcing, are more likely to be processed and retained than inconsistent messages. Our different backgrounds cause us to perceive messages in a different manner from others. Thus, we must become aware of the individuals with whom we are attempting to communicate and structure our messages for our specific audience in order to avoid selective exposure, selective attention, selective perception, or selective retention. Such avoidance can only occur when we have a reasonably good understanding of the listener's background and construct messages to reflect that background.

3.7 Oral messages that we receive and process but that are inconsistent with our attitudes tend to create cognitive dissonance within us.

The basic assumption underlying dissonance theory is that an individual strives for consistency among his or her opinions, attitudes, and values. Festinger (1957) replaced the word "consistency" with the more neutral term "consonance" and the word "inconsistency" with the more neutral term "dissonance." Basically, dissonance theory contends that we experience a pressure to produce consonant relationships among our cognitions—knowledge, beliefs, attitudes, values that we hold about ourselves or our environment—and thus attempt to avoid dissonant relations.

When we receive and process oral messages inconsistent with our opinions, attitudes, and values, we experience dissonance. For example, if a speaker were to tell a high school graduate that a university education is tremendously important for success just after she has decided not to attend college and, instead, to accept a job as a saleswoman, she would probably experience dissonance. This dissonance is assumed to cause psychological discomfort, which drives the individual to try to reduce inconsistency and to achieve consonance. Expectations about what cognitive relationships are consonant are acquired through an individual's experience, the mores of his or her culture, and his or her notions about logical relations between events.

When dissonance is created, it can be reduced in a variety of ways. For example, we might change the importance of consonant cognitions. This method is used by the individual who, rather than stop smoking cigarettes in the face of their known dangers to health, increases the feeling of enjoyment the habit brings. The smoker might also add new consonant elements, such as "Smoking is not so deadly as some people suggest—I run a far greater risk when I drive a car." Another method of reducing dissonance is to remove the dissonant elements. The smoker could give up smoking and thereby remove one major dissonance-producing element. Or, he or she could attempt to minimize another element, the claims of medical research, by distorting or ignoring them or, perhaps, by avoiding articles or arguments discussing the ill effects of smoking. In any event, most of us will find some method of eliminating or reducing the dissonance that messages inconsistent with our beliefs and attitudes cause.

Abstract

Judson Mills, "Changes in Moral Attitudes Following Temptation," *Journal of Personality,* Vol. 26 (1958), pp. 517–531.

Mills attempted to find answers to these two questions: (1) Will a person who succumbs to temptation and commits an act he considers immoral have less dissonance the greater the reward he gains? (2) Will a person who resists temptation have more dissonance the greater the reward he forsakes? An experiment with sixth graders was designed to find possible answers to these questions. The subjects were first given a questionnaire to measure the severity of their attitudes toward cheating. They then participated in a contest in which they worked individually at a task involving eye–hand coordination. Three experimental conditions were created: (1) high temptation to cheat (offer of a large prize for outstanding performance) together with low restraints against cheating (the students were given the chance to cheat while scoring their own performance); (2) low temptation (small prize) together with low restraint; and (3) high temptation together with high restraint (little opportunity to cheat). Some students cheated; some did not. A day later, the students were again asked about their attitudes toward cheating.

The findings generally supported dissonance theory. Attitude-change scores showed on the average that those children who cheated tended to become lenient toward cheating and that those who did not cheat became more critical of cheating.

Students who cheated for a small prize became more lenient toward cheating than did those who cheated for a big prize. Among the students who did not cheat, those who gave up a large prize became more severe in their condemnation of cheating than did those who gave up only a small one. Finally, the study showed that the effects of dissonance arousal are limited to cognitions directly relevant to the decisions involved. Attitudes were also measured by other aggressive actions unrelated to cheating, but these attitudes were unaffected by the experiment.

■ Messages that are inconsistent with attitudes will tend to create cognitive dissonance. When such dissonance occurs, individuals will find ways of reducing or eliminating it. In those situations where change is desired, it may be necessary first to create dissonance so that the individuals involved will be motivated to change. However, the desired change must be perceived as a reasonable way of eliminating the dissonance created by the inconsistent message.

Summary

The reception and processing of messages is a complex task. Many factors—most of which exist within the individual and are not directly available to the sender or source of the message—influence the manner in which such receiving and processing are done. However, the behavior of the source and the nature of the message can influence the manner in which it is received and processed. A moderate rate of speaking will enhance the reception of messages. It is important that this rate be slow enough to be comprehended easily, fast enough to keep the audience's attention and varied enough to make it interesting. A listener's ability to receive messages and to process them is influenced by his intelligence, his scholastic aptitude, and his vocabulary. Each of these characteristics directly influences the individual's ability to listen perceptively. If the listener is motivated to obtain information from the message, then reception of the message will be enhanced. Oral messages can also be enhanced when their nonverbal and verbal aspects are interrelated in such a way that they support and reinforce one another. The opportunity both to see and hear the speaker improves the efficiency and effectiveness of listening. The reinforcement of a speaker's ideas either through rhetorical devices such as illustration, repetition, or restatement, or through actively involving the listener with the message will increase the retention of the ideas being presented. Finally, the consistency of messages with existing attitudes, beliefs, experiences, and backgrounds influences the way in which we receive, process, and respond to messages. When the messages are inconsistent, we either attempt to avoid them or find ways to reduce the dissonance produced by them. When they are consistent, we are more likely to seek them out and to listen attentively to them.

Background Readings

Messages and relationships constitute the content and substance of human communication. Messages consist of people, objects, and events that are interpreted and given meaning. We process messages through our information system primarily by means of sight and sound, although other modes of sensing can be important. These readings provide background on listening, words, and actions.

Barker, Larry L., *Listening Behavior* (Englewood Cliffs, N. J.: Prentice-Hall, 1971). This book contains theory and a section on improving your listening behavior. A chapter on listening to biased communication includes a discussion of rumor.

Condon, John C., Jr., *Semantics and Communication* (New York: The Macmillan Co., 1966). This is a small book on how our language symbolizes experience, how it communicates meaning, and how it influences how we receive and process messages.

Harrison, Randall P., *Beyond Words: An Introduction to Nonverbal Communication* (Englewood Cliffs, N. J.: Prentice-Hall, 1974). This is an introductory book about how we interpret nonverbal cues and create meaning.

Knapp, Mark L., *Nonverbal Communication in Human Interaction* (New York: Holt, Rinehart and Winston, 1972). This is a broad survey of research and principles on nonlanguage aspects of communication. Space, appearance, physical behavior, face and eyes, and vocal cues are all discussed in separate chapters.

Mehrabian, Albert, *Silent Messages* (Belmont, Calif.: Wadsworth Publishing Co., 1971). In a brief and easy-to-read text, the author covers a wide range of nonverbal research and relates nonverbal behavior to basic human feelings and attitudes, especially liking, power, and responsiveness.

Sondel, Bess, *The Humanity of Words* (Cleveland, Ohio: World Publishing Co., 1958). This is an analysis and evaluation of three significant points of view concerning language in communication—*The Meaning of Meaning* by Ogden and Richards, *Science and Sanity* by Korzybski, and *Signs, Language and Behavior* by Morris. It represents, probably, the best summary of those theories in a nontechnical but accurate manner.

Travers, Robert M. W., *Man's Information System* (Scranton, Pa.: Chandler Publishing Company, 1970). This book is described as a "primer for media specialists," and it represents a practical review of how people create information out of raw perceptual data. One of the best statements on how our sensory systems influence what we know.

Weaver, Carl H., *Human Listening: Processes and Behavior* (Indianapolis: The Bobbs-Merrill Co., 1972). This is a comprehensive review of the principles of human listening and ways by which listening can be improved. A chapter on what both a listener and a talker can do to help improve listening is direct and practical.

4.1 Major ideas in messages are more easily comprehended than the details.

4.2 Oral messages that contain an apparent order are not necessarily more easy to comprehend; however, organization in written messages does enhance comprehension.

4.3 Messages employing emotional appeals are sometimes more effective than those employing rational appeals; however, effectiveness depends on both the type of message and audience.

4.4 Arguments presented at the beginning or the end of a message tend to be remembered better than those presented in the middle.

4.5 Messages that employ fear-arousing appeals tend to be more effective when the strength of the appeal is comparable with the importance of the issue in the receiver's mind.

4.6 Messages that initially express some views also held by the audience tend to be more effective.

4.7 The method of presenting an oral message can affect comprehension and influence audience interest. More effective presentation tends to be varied, flexible, animated, and direct.

4.8 Messages that tend to be interesting are more likely to cause attitude change than uninteresting ones. However, initial evidence seems to indicate that humor does not appear to be a particularly effective persuasive technique.

Chapter 4
Message Preparation and Presentation

As we consider the best ways to approach communicative situations, we are confronted with a variety of questions. We wonder how we can prepare oral messages to enhance the retention of information or to increase the likelihood of achieving a desired result. After this preparation we are concerned about the effective means of presenting them. This chapter will not even attempt to answer all the questions we might ask ourselves as we prepare or present a speech; however, it will attempt to cover some of the more common questions, such as: Should major ideas be given special stress? Does careful, logical organization make a speech more acceptable to the audience? Are rational or emotional appeals likely to be more persuasive? Where should the most important arguments occur during the presentation? Should appeals to fear be used? What aspects of delivery are important and in what ways? Obviously, the answers to such questions are important to understanding message preparation and presentation.

Predictive Propositions

4.1   Major ideas in messages are more easily comprehended than the details.

The major ideas we present as we speak to others will most likely be retained and remembered much longer than the details used to enhance them. Research in this area seems clearly to support this proposition. For example, Charles Petrie (1963), in reviewing research dealing with this proposition, concluded that "the rhetorical principle that a speech should be built around a few well-developed ideas is partially supported." Joseph Treneman (1951) also found that at every educational level tested the principal teaching points (the major ideas) were recalled more frequently than the other points. In fact, it appears that if the major ideas are clearly stated, the supporting details may be relatively unimportant. The following abstract exemplifies this.

Abstract

William A. Freedman, "A Study in Communication," *Journal of Communication,* Vol. 9 (1959), pp. 27–31.

Freedman was concerned with determining whether or not teaching time could be saved by the use of abstracted information without sacrificing comprehension and retention. More particularly, he attempted to discover whether or not using only the major ideas would significantly affect the retention of information. Two articles from an aircraft company's publication were used as expository communications. Three lengths of each article were used: full length, half length, and one-sixth length. Subjects then read each article in the differing lengths. Comprehension was measured with 13 true-false questions. Reading speed was also measured by having the subjects mark how far they had read each time after three minutes. However, they were then allowed to continue reading.

As the articles became shorter the subjects' reading speed decreased. However, they retained equivalent amounts of information for the three lengths of each article. The elimination of details did not seem significantly to affect the retention of the main ideas.

■ This particular study seems to suggest that when a speech is cut to bare essentials there is no less communication or retention of the main ideas. This seems to reinforce the idea that major ideas are remembered while minor details have less retention value. Thus, it would appear that, in preparing any message, we should determine which specific ideas we want our audience to remember and then make certain these ideas are presented as our main points and do not get lost in the details.

4.2   Oral messages that contain an apparent order are not necessarily more easy to comprehend; however, organization in written messages does enhance comprehension.

Judging from the amount of time and effort given to teaching organization, we doubt this proposition will be popular with some teachers of speech communication. However, the bulk of research done with oral communication and organization indicates that the organization of a speech has less effect on how well a person comprehends and retains it than we might have thought. The implication is not that speakers should neglect organization but, rather, as Thompson has stated, that "the speaker should not spend so much time and effort on organization that he sacrifices the attainment of other strong qualities. Similarly, teachers should avoid over-emphasis" (Thompson, 1967, p. 68).

Even though comprehension in oral communication does not seem to depend on the organization of materials, in written communication such organization seems definitely to enhance retention. Much of the research in this area is consistent with our proposition; however, one study, at least, differs. Ernest Thompson (1960) found that organization in oral communication helped with the retention of material but did not affect the persuasive impact of the message. This difference in findings indicates further need for research in this area before we make conclusive decisions about the effect of organization. The majority of studies, however, do indicate the lack of primary importance of organization in oral communication.

Since this proposition deals with both written and oral communication, it might be useful to look at abstracts of two different studies.

Abstract

John P. Parker, "Some Organizational Variables and Their Effect upon Comprehension," *Journal of Communication*, Vol. 12 (1962), pp. 27–32.

Parker's concern was with determining the effect of varying organizational patterns of factual prose. To analyze how different organizational patterns might affect comprehension, he constructed 16 variant forms of a 2,000 word pamphlet on opium. These 16 forms included all possible combinations of four factors: topic sentences, crossheadings, beginning summaries, and concluding summaries. Using a 24-item multiple choice test, he measured the comprehension of the subjects in his study. Some responded to the test immediately after reading the communication while others responded to the test one week later. Subjects were also asked to respond to a questionnaire assessing attitudes on the interestingness and organizational qualities of the pamphlet.

The use of topic sentences increased comprehension when the subjects were tested immediately. However, it did not seem to have any significant effect when one week had elapsed between reading the pamphlet and taking the test. The same was bound to be true of concluding summaries. They led to maximum comprehension when the material was tested immediately, but were less important when time had elapsed before taking the test. Opening summaries did not seem to enhance comprehension either immediately or after the one-week period.

Abstract

Donald K. Darnell, "The Relation between Sentence Order and Comprehension," *Speech Monographs*, Vol. 30 (1963), pp. 97–100.

Darnell was concerned with the question of order and its effect on comprehension in oral communication. In this study, he attempted to discover whether or not the creation of disorganization by taking a message consisting of sentences in a "because" or deductive order and mixing them up systematically so as to move each succeeding arrangement as far from the "right" order as possible would reduce the accuracy of respondents' predictions about the missing parts of the message. In this study the independent variable was sentence order. The experimental message consisted of (1) a thesis statement, (2) two major contentions, (3) two major subcontentions for each, and (4) two assertions for each subpoint (fifteen sentences in all). Seven treatment conditions were used in which the sentence orders were rearranged. For example, in the second treatment the thesis sentence was moved to the middle of the message.

■ The study determined that the comprehension scores for the seven forms of the message were so significantly different that the tentative conclusion might be that disorder can affect comprehension adversely and that the loss of clarity becomes greater as the degree of disorganization increases. In other words, although order may not be a major consideration in oral communication, good organization combined with emphasis on major ideas may effectively enhance the retention of orally produced materials. It is certainly clear that order is an important consideration in written communication.

4.3   Messages employing emotional appeals are sometimes more effective than those employing rational appeals; however, effectiveness depends on both the type of message and audience.

Many teachers of communication stress that a logically developed and supported presentation has a more persuasive impact on listeners than an emotional presentation. On the other hand, a good many lecturers appear to be much more effective when they load their presentation with largely emotional appeals. Research dealing with the use of emotional and logical appeals remains somewhat contradictory, perhaps because relatively little has been done in this area.

As early as the 1930s Hartman (1936) conducted a study on the influence of emotional-versus-factual appeals on voting behavior. He prepared two leaflets that asked voters to cast their ballots for Socialist Party candidates. The emotional leaflet dealt with the terrible consequences that would follow the election if Socialist Party candidates were not elected. Factual leaflets simply outlined the Socialist Party platform. In the city where the experiment was performed, a third of the voters were given emotional leaflets, a third were given factual leaflets, and the last third were given no leaflets and used as a control group. Socialist candidates did better in all wards in 1936 than they had in previous years. However, wards where the emotional leaflet was sent out showed the greatest increase in Socialist votes over the previous election. Wards where the factual leaflet was sent showed the next greatest increase. The wards receiving neither leaflet showed the least increase (Karlins and Abelson, 1970, p. 35). Other research in this same area is contradictory. Weiss (1960) conducted a study that determined rational appeals were more effective in persuading an audience than emotional. Carmichael and Cronkhite (1965) point out that the effectiveness of a particular appeal sometimes depends on the momentary mood of a given audience. It may be that emotional appeals are more effective in one situation while rational appeals are more effective in another.

The confusion existing about the effectiveness of these two approaches to persuasion may result from our inability to distinguish between emotional and rational appeals. For example, if we say that 100 children are dying from a particular disease, it is difficult to determine whether this is a rational appeal because it cites a specific number of individuals as victims of a disease or whether it is an emotional appeal because it speaks of dying children. Perhaps we should at least consider the possibility that no meaningful distinction can be made on the basis of the appeal itself. The difference may be in the meaning assigned to the information by the receiver, which the sender of the message cannot control to any great extent.

Abstract

Walter Weiss, "Emotional Arousal and Attitude Change," *Psychological Reports,* Vol. 6 (1960), pp. 267–280.

As with other research in this area, this study was an attempt to determine the relative influence on attitudes when emotionally appealing material is added to a rationally organized, persuasive message. Weiss also wanted to explore the relative effectiveness of a message designed to appeal solely to the recipients' emotions and to discover the relative effectiveness of several kinds of messages on retention.

Three groups of subjects read an article whose explicit conclusion was that criminals should be sternly and severely punished for their crimes. Group 1 read a communication containing a series of moderately detailed instances of violent and, at times, revolting crimes. Each example emphasized the horror of the particular crime and ended with the explicit remark or obvious implication that the criminal got less than "his due." The article ended with an open appeal for harsher treatment of criminals. Group 2 read a communication containing data, reasoned arguments, and rational principles to support the same point of view and conclusion but did not contain any specific examples. Group 3 first read the emotional appeal, then the rational appeal. The subjects responded to a questionnaire immediately after finishing reading and then again, two weeks later.

Answers showed that the emotionally charged article induced more emotional responses than did the primarily rational one. However, in terms of attitude change, the first group showed a significantly less punitive position than did the other two. In other words, the emotionally loaded message was less effective in changing attitudes in the desired direction. At the time of the second testing, two weeks later, the first two groups were not significantly different from each other in attitudes. However, they were significantly more punitive than the controlled subjects, indicating than any message was more effective than no message at all.

■ Obviously, more study is necessary in this area before any final conclusions can be reached. The present research is clearly contradictory. The differences between rational and emotional appeals have not been clearly drawn and the relative effectiveness of these two types of appeals, if they do exist as separate entities, has not been determined. In some situations the emotional appeal appears to be best; in others the rational appeal appears to be. Apparently, the situation and the audience dictate which appeal will be more effective.

4.4   Arguments presented at the beginning or the end of a message tend to be remembered better than those presented in the middle.

After reviewing a number of studies, Karlins and Abelson (1970) reported that without question arguments presented at the beginning or the end of a message tended to be remembered better than arguments presented in the middle. As a simple example of this, review the following list of nonsense syllables.

GAZ
TAY
BEK
WAD
FUX
SIZ
DOQ
TAZ
LUF
KIB

Give yourself three minutes to memorize the list and then see which syllables you remember best. Most of us will be better able to remember those items appearing at the beginning or the end of the list. This probably would be true about anything we might be asked to memorize, nonsense or not. Tannenbaum (1954) exposed 12 groups of subjects to 12 tape-recorded news broadcasts. Each broadcast consisted of 12 news items presented in a rotated sequence so that each group of subjects heard them in a different order. The position of each item in the broadcast determined how well it was remembered. Recall was better at either the beginning or the end of the newscast than it was in the middle.

When we have many ideas to present to others, it becomes difficult for our listeners to remember all of them. As a general rule, then, we may assume that if we want to construct an effective oral message that our audience will retain, we should make our most important points either at the beginning or the end of the presentation.

Abstract

Marvin E. Shaw, "A Serial Position Effect in Social Influence on Group Decisions." *Journal of Social Psychology,* Vol. 54 (1961), pp. 83–91.

This study concerned the effect order has on suggestions offered during group interaction. More specifically, Shaw asked whether the adoption of an individual's recommendation during a group discussion depended upon when it was stated. Data from two group decision-making studies were analyzed to examine the effect of order on such adoption. In both studies groups of four subjects were asked to solve problems through discussion and to try to reach consensus.

In the first study group decisions were almost always based on the first recommendation offered, regardless of who offered it. When an analysis was performed controlling for the number of opinions given, Shaw found that opinions stated first or last during the discussion had a significantly better chance of being adopted by the group than those offered sometime in-between. The second study, which was more carefully controlled than the first, reported similar findings. Thus, it became apparent in these studies that order or serial position influenced group decisions.

■ This proposition says a great deal to those who must prepare persuasive messages. The evidence is not clear, however, as to whether beginning or ending statements are more effective, but it does seem apparent that either is better than statements made in the middle of a presentation.

4.5 Messages that employ fear-arousing appeals tend to be more effective when the strength of the appeal is comparable with the importance of the issue in the receiver's mind.

On a recent late night talk show, one of the leading cancer researchers was being interviewed about the effect smoking has on lung cancer. He gave statistics dealing with the percentage of smokers who die of lung cancer and how many more smokers die of lung cancer than nonsmokers. The interviewer asked whether these statistics were not just a manipulation of numbers to make cigarette smoking seem much worse than it really is. Seemingly, he had been affected very little by the statistics presented. The researcher then began to describe in detail instances in which people died rather horrible deaths from lung cancer. At this point, and only then, did the interviewer act as if the researcher had said anything meaningful. The clincher came when the researcher claimed he had quit smoking because he enjoyed life too much to end it with tobacco. This appeal had such a visible effect on the interviewer that he even put out his cigarette. Even though this talk show does not rank as a scientific inquiry, still, most of the research conducted indicated that a fear-arousing message can be an important factor in persuading people. In earlier research Janis and Feshbach (1953), dealing with the importance of dental hygiene among students and types of messages that would best influence them to improve their dental hygiene habits, discovered that the more threatening the message the more the students expressed concern about better dental care. However, after a week the students who had received a mild fear appeal were conforming to the recommendations of the lecture more than those who had received a strong fear appeal.

Both mild and strong fear appeals do appear to be effective. It depends on the situation as to which is more effective. For example, Kraus and his associates (Kraus, El-Assal, and DeFleur, 1966) discovered that high fear appeals were more effective than moderate fear appeals. Fear appeals appear to be most effective in changing behavior when immediate action can be taken on the recommendations and when specific instructions are provided for carrying out the recommendations included in the appeal.

Abstract

James M. Dabbs and Howard Leventhal, "Effects of Varying the Recommendations in a Fear-Arousing Communication," *Journal of Personality and Social Psychology*, Vol. 4 (1966), pp. 525–531.

This study attempted to discover whether or not messages with high fear appeal would be more effective in changing attitudes and behavior than those with low fear appeal. The subjects were 182 Yale seniors who agreed to participate in a "student health survey," where they were presented with a pamphlet dealing with tetanus. The students were unaware that the researchers had systematically varied the contents of the booklets in the following three ways:

1. *Fear level of the message:* In the low-fear communication, tetanus was described as difficult to contract and relatively easy to cure. A case history, complete with black and white photographs, told of recovery from the disease following "mild medication and throat suction procedures." In the high-fear communication, tetanus was pictured as

easy to contract and difficult to cure. Another case study, this one with color pictures, described death from tetanus "despite heavy medication and surgery to relieve throat congestion." In a third, no fear message (controlled conditions) was included, and the discussion of tetanus and the accompanying case study were omitted from the pamphlets.

2. *Reported effectiveness of inoculation in preventing tetanus:* Two messages were presented—a low-effectiveness message and a high-effectiveness message.

3. *Reported painfulness of the inoculation:* Again, two messages were presented—a no-pain message and a high-pain message.

After reading the assigned pamphlet, each student filled out a questionnaire. To determine whether the students actually carried out their stated intentions in the questionnaire, the experimenters obtained an inoculation record for each subject at the university's health service.

The investigators were surprised to discover that no differences in shot-taking behavior existed between groups of students who were exposed to different information about how effective and how painful the inoculations would be. There was a difference, however, in student attitudes and behavior toward inoculations based on the fear appeal they had read. Those exposed to the high-fear communication were much more likely to want shots and actually to get them than the individuals receiving the low-fear communication. A positive relationship, then, between persuasion and fear arousal was observed.

■ The use of fear appeals seems to be an effective means of persuading people to change their attitudes and their behavior concerning an issue. However, the effectiveness of such an appeal appears to depend on the audience, the situation, and its strength as a fear appeal. On some occasions high-fear appeals will be most effective, on other occasions moderate-fear appeals will be most effective. However, in most situations some fear appeal will be more effective than none whatsoever.

4.6   Messages that initially express some views also held by the audience tend to be more effective.

The technique of "flogging a dead horse" has been used by most public speakers at one time or another. The idea here is to present a position to an audience that agrees with one they already hold. After making this presentation, we can then make our persuasive plea. Most research on this topic appears to demonstrate that such an approach is effective.

Such strategy was illustrated a number of years ago when Senator Robert F. Kennedy spoke to the student body of Brigham Young University. The speech he gave was made about two weeks after he had announced his candidacy for the presidency. He knew at this point in the campaign that his main opponent was President Johnson and was also aware that his predominantly liberal views would probably conflict with the rather conservative views held by the students. Therefore, he spent his first ten minutes discussing an army—called Johnson's Army—that was sent against the Mormons in Utah in the early history of the territory. After establishing his knowledge of the history of Utah, he stated he felt just like one of the Mormons who was forced to fight against Johnson's Army. This remark brought a great roar of approval before Kennedy launched into discussing why the troops should come home from Vietnam, a point of view his audience did not necessarily hold. But attitude scales administered before and after his presentation indicated a significant shift of opinion toward Kennedy's position (Peterson, 1968).

Thus, by establishing agreement with an audience on the first issue, the speaker puts a damper on the critical capacities of the audience before presenting the next—thus increasing the likelihood that they will accept the second position as well. However, it is vital that the presentation following the "dead horse" issue be well prepared and quite persuasive. If not, such an effort will have little effect, even with using the "dead horse" approach.

Abstract

Walter Weiss, "Opinion Congruence with a Negative Source on One Issue as a Factor Influencing Agreement on Another Issue," *Journal of Abnormal and Social Pscyhology,* Vol. 54 (1957), pp. 180–186.

Weiss was interested in determining whether an audience could be made to accept a point of view on a particular subject more easily if the speaker also expressed other opinions known to agree with what the audience already believed. He chose the issue of fluoridation of drinking water to persuade the audience of its negative effects, and for the "dead horse" issue he selected the topic of academic freedom because the students, who were the subjects in his experiment, were almost unanimously and strongly in favor of it. Some students were presented first with the message on academic freedom, then with the message on fluoridation.

Others were exposed to a neutral message followed by the message on fluoridation. All groups filled out an opinion questionnaire after the presentation.

The group receiving the "dead horse" treatment were won over to the desired viewpoint on the fluoridation issue more often than the groups that did not receive that approach.

■ Apparently, when we communicate with an audience we really wish to impress or persuade, it is important that we initially present a message agreeing with some of their strongly held beliefs. Such initial agreement will help create a more favorable reception of the more controversial idea we present next. However, if we expect to influence our audience, this presentation must be as persuasive as we can make it.

4.7 The method of presenting an oral message can affect comprehension and influence audience interest. More effective presentation tends to be varied, flexible, animated, and direct.

The method of presenting an oral message (delivery) has concerned students of communication since the earliest times. A number of individuals have studied the effects of delivery. Bettinghaus (1961) stated that "effectiveness in delivery contributes not only to the credibility of the speaker, but also to the persuasiveness of the speaker in achieving acceptance of his message." Vohs (1964) discovered that "good delivery did produce significantly higher retention scores, and for the most complex task it also increased the information handling capacity of the listener." Most of the research indicates that as a general rule delivery does greatly affect audience interest. In fact, Wayne Thompson (1967) concludes:

Every study of the relation of delivery or of any of its aspects to some desirable outcome arrives at the same conclusion: good delivery does matter. Such unanimity is unusual in the behavioral sciences, where the complexity of the variables and the test situations makes nonsignificant and conflicting findings common (p. 84).

There is, however, some disagreement. Occasional studies have pointed out that delivery may not have much effect on comprehension. Diehl, White, and Satz (1961) discovered that a person presenting a message in a monotonous delivery was rated as a significantly poorer speaker than persons who used appropriate inflection at intervals. Delivery did not, however, seem to affect comprehension.

Although the research seems clearly to indicate that delivery affects audience interest and satisfaction, some disagreement exists as to just *how* it affects comprehension. Such problems as a speaker might have with nonfluency, poor pitch, or undesirable quality might be considered unpleasant by an audience while not necessarily harming the comprehension of his message. The following study is an example of such research.

Abstract

Charles F. Diehl, Richard C. White, and Paul H. Satz, "Pitch Change and Comprehension," *Speech Monographs*, Vol. 28 (March 1961), pp. 65–68.

This study was concerned directly with the effect that changes in a speaker's pitch might have on listeners' comprehension. A 14-minute informative lecture on "Birds" (a topic about which it was believed members of the experimental groups would have little knowledge) was prepared and taped. This tape, judged as representing effective use of interval and inflection, was called the control tape. To measure the effectiveness of interval and inflection on listener comprehension, the control tape was varied by eliminating all interval and inflection while keeping other voice variables constant. Immediately after hearing the recorded lecture, subjects completed a two-part test, which also included a measure of their reactions to the "quality" of the delivery.

In this study no significant differences were found on the subjects' comprehension scores. However, ratings of the delivery were between "very good" and "good" for the group hearing the lecture with normal use of interval and inflection and close to "poor" for the group hearing the lecture with all interval and inflection eliminated. The indication is that the use of interval and inflection does not affect listener comprehension, but does appear to affect listener perception of the quality of the delivery. Seemingly, listeners prefer listening to a speaker who uses appropriate interval and inflection.

■ From what we can discover, all aspects of delivery appear to be crucial in the oral presentation of messages since they affect how an audience responds to a speaker. Some question may exist as to whether delivery has a direct effect on retaining information from the speech. However, little reason appears to exist for questioning that varied, flexible, animated, and direct delivery does assist in maintaining listener interest. The next proposition may help us to realize whether or not interest is important.

4.8 Messages that tend to be interesting are more likely to cause attitude change than uninteresting ones. However, initial evidence seems to indicate that humor does not appear to be a particularly effective persuasive technique.

Perhaps the most difficult consideration here is what is interesting, since this seems to be a highly personal matter. What one person considers interesting may be completely boring to someone else. A message dealing with professional football may be highly interesting to you and equally repulsive to your friend. Our backgrounds, our prejudices, our perceptions, the situations in which we live, along with a myriad of variables, shape our ideas of what is interesting or uninteresting. But, regardless, the research seems to indicate that if a person perceives a message as interesting, he or she will more likely retain more of its meaning and change in the direction desired by the speaker. John Dietrich (1946) discovered that the amount of interest expressed is positively and significantly related to the effect a message has on influencing the subject's attitudes. Russel Windes (1961) discovered in evaluating presidential campaign speaking that those speeches that were effective contained 589 devices useful in promoting interest, while those speeches that were ineffective contained only 272 devices. Other researchers discovered that of two talks the more interesting would be more effective in producing goodwill, while audience members who indicated enjoying a speech were more persuasible than those who did not (Irwin and Brockhaus, 1963; Furbay, 1965).

Many of us have felt, especially in public speaking, that humor is a particularly good device for creating interest. For some reason, however, this has not been a topic subjected to much research. Perhaps we have been so sure that humor is effective that we have not bothered to find out whether it is. Interestingly, initial efforts in this area lead us to believe that humor is not the potent device in causing attitude change that we thought it to be. However, the research is very limited and final conclusions cannot be made. Charles Gruner (1965) has made some initial efforts in this area, particularly with satirical humor, and has discovered that such humor was not effective in causing people to change their attitudes.

Abstract

Charles R. Gruner, "An Experimental Study of Satire as Persuasion," *Speech Monographs,* Vol. 32 (June 1965) pp. 149–153.

This particular study was directly concerned with the use of satire as a means of changing attitudes. More specifically, it attempted to discover whether a speech satirizing censorship could be employed to change attitudes about censorship. Gruner developed a speech satirizing censorship that exaggerated its underlying rationale. With mock seriousness it urged that, since nursery rhymes are so obscene and excessively violent, they should be strictly censored.

To test the entertainment value of this speech, the writer checked on the manuscript those places where the audience responded with "general laughter," defined here as "at least half the group laughing audibly." All 7 groups of listeners responded with general laughter in 11 identical places, and at least 5 or 6 of the 7 groups responded in the same way in 8 other identical places. Nineteen such instances, along with many other scattered laughs and smiles, validated this speech as being "humorous." An attitude scale was administered before and after the speech. Ratings of "perceived intelligence of the speaker" and "perceived funniness of the speech" were also secured from the subjects.

Because the scores on the attitude scales did not change significantly, Gruner concluded that the censorship speech had no effect on subjects' attitudes. Although the censorship speech was very humorous, this humor seemingly had no direct effect on the subjects' attitudes toward the idea of censorship.

■ Whether materials are considered interesting obviously differs from individual to individual. However, the research in this area does lend itself to at least one conclusion: When subjects perceive a message as interesting, they tend to be more persuaded than when they perceive it as uninteresting. Retention does not seem to be directly affected by interestingness. Humor is an area that needs considerably more research, but initial studies seem to indicate that it is not a particularly effective means of persuasion.

Summary

Even though the research on preparing and presenting messages is not complete or decisive, it does provide some guidelines that we should keep in mind. Major ideas in a message seem to be more easily comprehended than the details and should, therefore, be emphasized. Organization is useful but is much more important in written than in oral messages. Emotional and rational appeals have not been clearly differentiated nor can we say which might be more effective. It is, however, apparent that the order in which arguments are presented does make a difference. Those presented at the beginning or at the end of a message are likely to be remembered better than those presented in the middle. Fear-arousing appeals can be effective but must be adapted to the topic, the audience, and the situation. They are most effective when immediate action can be taken and when specific instructions are provided for carrying out the recommendations. It is useful to express views your audience holds before expressing new views that you hope they will accept. Although delivery may not have an important effect on comprehension, it does help to make speeches more interesting; messages that are interesting are also more likely to cause a change in attitude than those that are not. Much research remains to be done in this area. Perhaps you will do some of it.

Background Readings

The question posed by this chapter is "How does one assemble and display verbal and nonverbal materials so as to create messages with clarity and impact?" These readings provide background on locating, structuring, and presenting information and evidence of both verbal and nonverbal types to achieve a purpose.

Bettinghaus, Erwin P., *Message Preparation: The Nature of Proof* (Indianapolis: The Bobbs-Merrill Co., 1966). This publication stresses the discovery of evidence and its arrangement for the creation of belief.

Bosmajian, Haig A., *The Rhetoric of Nonverbal Communication: Readings* (Glenview, Ill.: Scott, Foresman and Co., 1971). These readings focus on finding and using nonverbal means of persuasion. The intent is to show how nonverbal communication can be used purposefully.

Holtzman, Paul D., *The Psychology of Speakers' Audiences* (Glenview, Ill.: Scott, Foresman and Co., 1970). This book examines what people should know about audiences in order to prepare and present messages adequately.

LaRusso, Dominick, *Basic Skills of Oral Communication* (Dubuque, Iowa: Wm. C. Brown Co., 1967). This publication describes basic principles that underlie effective oral presentation of messages.

Mills, Glen E., *Message Preparation: Analysis and Structure* (Indianapolis: The Bobbs-Merrill Co., 1966). This volume treats the aspects of message preparation that concern how to select a subject, determine the purpose, analyze the subject, find information, and organize the materials.

Part 3
Information Diffusion

Shannon and Weaver (1949) observed that "information is a measure of one's freedom of choice when one selects a message." Information as used in this mathematical sense is concerned with the number of choices a person has in selecting a particular message—that is, the concern is more with what you could say and less with what is actually said. On the other hand, in everyday conversation, we usually say we have received information when we know something that we did not know before. We are concerned less with what could be said and more with what actually is said. Thus, information, as we employ the term, has to do with messages and knowledge about people, objects, and events.

Diffusion consists of the rather complex process of communicating information (messages and knowledge) to other people. Diffusion, however, not only implies simply communicating to others but suggests that information is spread widely among many individuals. That is, when information is diffused, messages are disseminated to large numbers of people, usually to members of formal organizations, residents of a community, audiences of individuals in face-to-face contact, or to groups of viewers, listeners, or readers who get the message over radio, television, or by some printed material.

Often the information to be diffused consists of messages about "new" ideas, products, or procedures. Rogers (1962) referred to the dissemination of messages about new ideas as "the diffusion of innovations." Wherever new ideas are involved, some type of change is anticipated. We will introduce propositions about change in Part Four. In this section we shall be concerned primarily with ways of diffusing information, the channels of communication, and the acquisition of new ideas. Considerations of attitude and behavioral change as a consequence of the information that has been diffused will be taken up in the next section. Propositions about three contexts in which information is diffused will be discussed: face-to-face groups, social groups, and serial groups. The setting in which the communication occurs can seriously influence the process. Information diffusion to face-to-face groups may be quite different from information diffusion to serial groups or social groups. Thus, we shall treat each of these unique settings in different chapters.

5.1 Giving a speech to an audience can be an effective method of diffusing information to a large face-to-face group.

5.2 A speech to a large face-to-face group can cause a significant change in the attitude of its members.

5.3 Information comprehension and/or attitude change brought about by public speaking are likely to become insignificant within a few short weeks following the speech if reinforcement is not provided.

5.4 A speech to an audience is likely to be more effective when the speaker can be seen and uses gestures and visual aids.

Chapter 5
Face-to-Face Groups

Often, when we think of communicating information to large groups of individuals, the mass media come to mind as the only means by which the process may occur. However, it is possible to communicate with quite a few people in a face-to-face situation. For example, if we consider an audience of 2,000 a large group, all over the nation we have convention speakers attempting to communicate information to large groups of people. As a rule, such speakers do use an amplifying system so their voices can be easily heard throughout the audience, but, usually, they do not employ other technological devices. Although we shall consider the influence of the media on information dissemination in the next chapter, here our major concern will be with those factors that influence the diffusion of information by a speaker that can see and be seen by the audience to whom he or she is talking.

In some situations the speech may also be carried by the mass media to other audiences. For example, when the president of the United States addresses a large convention, his speech will invariably be carried by the mass media as well. There are numerous other examples. However, for our purposes we will consider a large group of people as one in which there are sufficient numbers of individuals to impel a speaker to prepare his or her information in advance. Our focus will be on information diffusion in face-to-face situations in which the speaker presents organized information to a group of people who rarely, if ever, interrupt. In other words, we are talking about what has commonly been called public speaking. Examples of such situations would be lectures in classrooms, talks at conventions and conferences, oral technical reports, popular lectures at assemblies and convocations, addresses to juries, reports to stockholders, sermons to congregations, and commencement addresses.

Predictive Propositions

5.1 Giving a speech to an audience can be an effective method of diffusing information to a large face-to-face group.

The amount of information people acquire from a speech is often evaluated by measuring their knowledge of a subject before and after listening to informative speeches. In general, artistically excellent informative speeches tend to result in the retention of significant amounts of data and are effective in disseminating information to large face-to-face groups (McKeachie, 1963, pp. 1118–1172).

The informative speech or lecture has survived as a method of disseminating information to groups of people because the lecturer can provide a focus for the audience's attention and encourage listeners to persevere in seeking relevant information. The lecturer can also interpret, reiterate, guide the acquisition of information, or add an explanation that is unavailable from other fixed message sources. He can, because of his proximity to the audience, be aware of the need for further amplification, and satisfy that need immediately. He may also inspire listeners by his enthusiasm or through his method of delivering ideas. Tompkins and Samovar (1964) constructed a speech on the topic of medical care for the aged that 32 teachers of public speaking and 30 students in a course in public speaking judged to be "informative" (rather than persuasive). Regardless of whether the introduction of the speaker was favorable, unfavorable, or neutral, the speech resulted in a significant amount of learning. The study suggests that a public speech can be an effective way of disseminating information to a face-to-face group. Bloom (1953) studied thought processes during lectures and discussions and concluded that "the lecture is especially successful when securing the attention of students to what is being said, but it evokes primarily those thoughts which are appropriate to the following and comprehending of information." Apparently, the lecture can be effective for acquiring information. Some evidence suggests that the face-to-face public speech is more effective than more indirect methods such as the radio or printed text. Wilke (1934) compared the influence on audience attitudes of a speech given live with the same speech presented over a loudspeaker and then as a mimeographed or printed text that had been transcribed verbatim. Emotional propaganda on the topics of war, distribution of wealth, birth control, and the existence of God were used. The live speech had the most striking effect, the speech over the loudspeaker next, and the printed text last.

Abstract

Harry Ruja, "Outcomes of Lectures and Discussion Procedures in Three College Courses," *Journal of Experimental Education*, Vol. 22 (June 1954), pp. 385–394.

This study attempted to discover whether students in courses using discussion methods would show greater improvement than students in lecture courses in subject-matter mastery and emotional judgment, express more favorable attitudes toward their instructor, and become better acquainted with their classmates. Equal numbers of classes in psychology and philosophy were taught using lecture and discussion formats. Each course involved was thoroughly prepared in advance and standardized for a period of two semesters.

Students in the lecture sections were superior in subject-matter mastery as demonstrated by their scores on examinations. They also showed greater gains than students in discussion courses on the Bell Adjustment Inventory, a measure of emotional adjustment. The instructors were rated favorably in equal numbers of lecture and discussion sections. However, students in the discussion sections got to know one another in greater numbers than those in the lecture sessions.

■ Apparently, informative speeches, or lectures, can be an effective means of diffusing information to a face-to-face group. Because of the ability of the speaker to adjust and adapt to the particular needs of his audience, public speeches can result in a significant amount of learning. We should not overlook or diminish the importance of face-to-face formal public speaking as a way of communicating information. The development of skills in this form of communication has provided and will no doubt continue to provide widespread benefits for individuals and society.

5.2 A speech to a large face-to-face group can cause a significant change in the attitude of its members.

All of us have experienced listening to a speaker who caused us to change our basic attitudes about some topic. There have been numbers of such effective speakers throughout history. Some were able to effect beneficial change, others were able to lead mankind to less useful, sometimes disastrous activities. Adolf Hitler was a particularly effective public speaker. As he spoke, people screamed, shed tears, and threw their arms in the air. He motivated people to become the aggressors in war and to die for him and his promises. Although there has been very little research on the changes in attitudes caused by Hitler's speeches, the change in behavior of those to whom he spoke seems to indicate that they were persuaded to act. More recently, Thomas Dooley, the physician who founded village hospitals in Southeast Asia and organized a worldwide medical foundation called Medico, was able to influence the attitudes of those who heard him speak. Dooley did not use the same approach as Hitler. Quiet and sincere, he told emotional stories about his personal experiences, but the behavior of those who heard him speak would indicate he was impressive. Following his speeches, he collected thousands of dollars for Medico. More recently, in this country, we have all been made aware of agitators whose public speaking abilities have had the power to sway their listeners' attitudes and actions.

In the early 1940s, Gilkinson (1944) brought together the research that had been done on the persuasive effects of speakers on audiences. He made the following generalization:

It has been demonstrated repeatedly in aforementioned studies, as well as others, that public address influences significantly the attitudes and opinions of audiences. There is evidence that this effect is usually of the nature of a modification of degrees of favorableness and unfavorableness of attitude, rather than a winning of total converts.

According to Gilkinson, we are not necessarily influenced to change our behavior after hearing a public speech; however, our attitudes may change in varying degrees according to the speaking situation. Since Gilkinson's early survey, much research on modifying attitudes has been done. From it we are able to conclude in general that the public speaking format can be an effective aid in bringing about attitude change. Thistlethwaite, Kemenetzky, and Schmidt (1956) found in a study on the effectiveness of one-sided vs. two-sided speeches that both were effective in modifying attitude. Gulley and Berlo (1956) found when using differing types of message arrangement in a speaking situation that they all effected significant attitude changes. Irwin and Brockhaus (1963) found significant changes in an audience's attitudes as a result of a lecture situation. It seems apparent that lectures can result in changes in attitudes. It would be difficult to determine what particular aspect of the lecture is the primary influence, but it is even more difficult to deny that the lecture taken as a whole can and does result in attitude change.

Abstract

Thomas S. Ludlum, "The Effects of Certain Techniques of Credibility upon Audience Attitude," *Speech Monographs,* Vol. 25 (Nov. 1958), pp. 278–284.

Ludlum attempted to determine whether credibility would increase the persuasability of an argumentative speech to an audience. He prepared eight speeches concerning the 1956 general election. They presented contentions dealing with three major issues: (1) Are the Republican agricultural policies preferable to the Democratic agricultural policies? (2) Are the Republican school policies preferable to those of the Democrats? (3) Are the Republican fiscal policies preferable to those of the Democrats? Five aspects of credibility were built into four of the speeches and the other four were straight argumentative speeches. The subjects used in this study were college students enrolled in speech courses. Most of them were freshmen and sophomores, with some juniors and seniors participating along with a few graduate students. In the experimental groups 620 subjects served, and in the control group 100 served. An attitude scale was prepared to measure audience responses to the speeches. A pretest was given to both the experimental and the control group after which members of the experimental groups heard one of the speeches. Both the experimental and the control groups then received a posttest.

The study results demonstrated that a significant change in attitudes can be brought about by exposing subjects to a brief oral argument in the form of a public speech. The 620 experimental subjects who heard political speeches made a significantly greater mean shift in the desired direction than did the control group.

■ The political speaker may find that those techniques commonly recognized as contributing to credibility for general communication have little real value for him. A straightforward argumentative approach was discovered in this study to be more effective in political speaking. However, regardless of which speech was heard, shifts in attitude did occur.

5.3   Information comprehension and/or attitude change brought about by public speaking are likely to become insignificant within a few short weeks following the speech if reinforcement is not provided.

Although many speakers seem to have an immediate impact on an audience, the impact may not continue over a long period of time unless some means of reinforcement is provided. Without reinforcement, there is an excellent chance that information will be forgotten and that attitudes will regress toward the former ones. In an early study Knower, Phillips, and Keoppel (1945) found that in an informative speaking situation, subjects forgot a significant amount of information after a four-week period. However, in this same study the subjects also remembered a significant amount of information. Cromwell (1954) found the immediate shift of opinion caused by a persuasive lecture does not necessarily persist; after a period of time the audience's attitude regressed toward the original one.

Since most of the research in this area is done in experimental studies, the results may not always be the same in an actual speaking situation. The research does seem to indicate that much information in a speech is lost over time if it is not reinforced. In summarizing this research, Thompson (1967) observes:

The temporary nature of results obtained experimentally does not mean, however, that informative and persuasive efforts are always useless. Lasting effects are not always essential to a speaker's purpose, and moreover, experimental and real life conditions probably differ importantly in respect to reinforcement. Whereas topics in investigations are chosen so as to minimize contamination from outside influences, reinforcement is almost always present in such realistic situations as advertising, political campaigns, formal and informal speech making in behalf of causes, and person-to-person efforts in home or office (pp. 44–45). Such reinforcement may take place in a variety of ways, including such methods as repeating the original message or involving audience members in activities related to the topic.

Abstract

Harvey Cromwell, "The Persistency of the Effect of Argumentative Speeches," *Quarterly Journal of Speech,* Vol. 41 (April 1955), pp. 154–158.

Cromwell was directly concerned with discovering how long-lasting a shift in audience attitude obtained by an argumentative speech might be. Specifically, he tried to discover whether or not the shift would persist after a period of 30 days. Data were collected on 1,319 students enrolled in the basic speech course at two different universities. An affirmative and a negative speech were prepared on two propositions: (1) The federal government should provide medical care for everyone; and (2) the federal government should require arbitration of labor disputes. Each speech was recorded by a male speaker and subsequently replayed in experimental situations. A control group and an experimental group were used. The experimental group was given an attitude pretest, a speech, an attitude posttest, and 30 days later the second attitude posttest.

The control group took all the tests but did not hear the speech.

The argumentative speeches were strongly effective in producing significant shifts in listeners' attitudes toward the side advocated by the speaker. After 30 days, auditors who heard strong argumentative speeches regressed toward their original attitudes, but they were still influenced by the speeches. The evidence also indicated that the stronger the immediate effectiveness of the argumentative speech, the greater the influence it exercised on the listeners' attitudes after 30 days.

■ It is apparent that public speeches can have significant effects on acquiring information and on shifts in attitude. However, when a speaker wishes to have a lasting persuasive effect on an audience or wishes his audience to gain and retain information over a period of time, he should be aware that the impact of persuasion and the retention of information subside at a rapid rate following the speech. If we wish to be most effective, we must reinforce our presentation so that it will have a lasting impact. In real life, reinforcement usually exists. For example, in a political campaign we hear continual speeches, see advertisements, are subjected to mass media campaigns, and become involved in discussions with other persons. Such reinforcement is essential for long-term effectiveness.

5.4 A speech to an audience is likely to be more effective when the speaker can be seen and uses gestures and visual aids.

Audiences like to be able to see the speakers. They enjoy the speeches more and retain information more when they can see the speaker's bodily actions, gestures, and facial expressions (Ewbank, 1932). In addition, audiences seem to comprehend significantly more when they can see the speaker rather than simply hear him (Kramar and Lewis, 1951). The use of visual aids can also increase listener comprehension (Knower, Phillips, and Keoppel, 1945; Ulrich, 1957). Most writers about public speaking have indicated that visual aids are good reinforcers and positively influence an audience to retain information. In short, much of the research and writing on public speaking suggests that the use of both the visual and aural channels enhances a person's ability to learn and comprehend information in a public speaking situation.

Abstract

Edward J. Kramar and Thomas R. Lewis, "Comparison of Visual and Nonvisual Listening," *Journal of Communication,* Vol. 1 (Nov. 1951), pp. 16–20.

Kramar and Lewis were directly interested in determining whether there would be a difference in listening ability between two groups of students when one group saw and heard the speaker and the other only heard the speaker. They were attempting to discover whether the element of visual cues in the face-to-face situation was an aid to understanding and retaining expository materials. A lecture was delivered in a small theatre divided into two sections by a heavy curtain with a loudspeaker placed on each side of the room. The speaker's stand was placed on the right side of the theatre so that only the group on that side both saw and heard the speaker. Arm-and-hand gestures, facial expressions, and head and body movements were introduced to add naturalness to the delivery. Following the lecture, the two groups answered a multiple choice test on the content.

Results indicated that the visual group had a greater range of scores than the nonvisual group. The differences between the means of the two groups were significant beyond the 1% level of confidence. Thus, this study suggests that the speaker's visible presence and action contributed to the listener's ability to understand and remember the ideas expressed.

■ The speaker who desires to make the best possible impression on an audience should speak to them in person, have effective physical delivery, and perhaps use good visual aids. Combining the visual and aural channels will likely enhance the audience's retention of information.

Summary

Public speaking to face-to-face groups is used extensively in our society. It can be an effective method of diffusing information to a large group of individuals, often providing greater retention of information as well as more satisfaction on the part of the listeners. It can, in addition, result in a significant change of attitudes among members of the audience. However, both the retention of information and the change in attitudes are likely to diminish significantly over a period of time unless some means is found to reinforce the ideas presented. Without reinforcement the impact is significantly less. The physical presence of the speaker is an essential ingredient of effective face-to-face communication with large groups. The speaker is likely to be considerably more effective when he or she can be seen and is physically active, using gestures and, perhaps, visual aids. The mass media are not the only means of communicating information to large groups of individuals. Public speaking can also be effective.

Background Readings

Available material on speaking to groups is myriad, ranging from small pocket-books to massive handbooks. The approach is usually rhetorical rather than scientific. These books follow the classical tradition but provide a solid overview of concepts and practices that lead to effective informative speaking to audiences.

Howell, William S., and Ernest G. Bormann, *Presentational Speaking for Business and the Professions* (New York: Harper & Row, 1971). Part Two analyzes the techniques of making presentations in the context of business. The primary focus is on securing acceptance, but the methods described are informational.

Monroe, Alan H., and Douglas Ehninger, *Principles of Speech Communication,* 6th Brief ed. (Glenview, Ill.: Scott, Foresman and Co., 1969). This book has been one of the most widely used and consulted references on public speaking since the 1940s. It represents a solid exposition of the principles involved in speaking to large audiences.

Olbricht, Thomas H., *Informative Speaking* (Glenview, Ill.: Scott, Foresman and Co., 1968). This small paperback treats the topic of information diffusion through speaking to face-to-face audiences.

Rogge, Edward, and James C. Ching, *Advanced Public Speaking* (New York: Holt, Rinehart and Winston, 1966). This is one of the few books that devotes discussion to presenting abstracts, instructions, informal and technical reports, and lectures.

6.1 The network of acquaintances is such that the odds are good (about 50-50) that two people can be linked by two intermediate acquaintances; this small world concept increases the likelihood that information will spread quite widely.

6.2 The diffusion of information on a wide scale occurs through the communication facilities of the mass media.

6.3 Word-of-mouth communication informs potential buyers, circulates rumors, and operates the grapevine.

6.4 The communication network—who can talk to whom—affects the efficiency of information diffusion and the morale of members of the network.

Chapter 6
Social Groups

Communication is the central feature of all human relationships; without it, organized social activities are impossible. It is easy to demonstrate that the successful completion of large categories of tasks depends upon having an adequate flow of information among those involved. Whenever the task must be performed by a number of people rather than a single individual, diffusion of information among the group members is essential to coordinated effort. Information can be made available only so far as they have effective channels for communication. For example, a group member who does not talk to other members is of necessity isolated from that particular group. On the other hand, an individual who talks only to members of one group is restricted to that group for information. The pattern of information flow among members of various social groups indicates the structure of social relationships in organizations and communities. Knowing something about who gets information from whom or what allows us not only to understand the processes by which people adopt new ideas and practices but also who influences what happens in a group, organization, or community and the conditions under which rumor, propaganda, and advertising are most effective. In this chapter, we will focus on the flow of information in groups—both large and small—and then, in the next chapter, examine the factors that influence the way information is reproduced in a person-to-person-to-person network.

Through technologies of the print and electronic media, a person can receive information from all parts of the country and the world, often as the event is actually occurring. In addition, through the facilities of video and audio tapes, we have access to the sights and sounds of memorable events of the past. The telephone is a major vehicle for private communication, in some instances replacing even the letter for communicating information that in the past was handled through the mails. As a matter of fact, telephone networks are actually engineered, through the use of private lines, to optimize private and selective communication between two individuals. Goldmark (1972) even suggests that it is possible with current technology to envision an "interactive home terminal consisting of a television receiver, a voice response computer and various combinations of keyboards, light pens, printers and electronic logic and storage systems." By combining the concepts of the telephone and cable television, it is possible to have a "full, two-way, random access network that can accommodate voice, data, and pictures." That is, we have the ability to connect every home, office, school, library, and work area so that we can not only converse but also receive and transmit written materials and pictures. Such a system could put any individual in personal contact with anyone or anything else in a quick and reliable manner. Thus, we have the ultimate in mass but personal information distribution. In cities it is possible to place in each home a broad band, two-way information cable with a capacity equivalent to 30 or more television channels. Such a system would allow cities to obtain information about individual needs, then process and move that information to the individuals who can use it, rather than trying to move people and materials to the information.

With the ability to interconnect people with cables giving access to information, it is possible to control what kinds of information will be available through those connections. Such developments have not only extended the ability of human beings to exchange information but have also transformed the very environment in which the human consciousness is born and cultivated. With more information available, individuals must eventually decide which kinds of information they will seek and want.

The propositions that follow are more descriptive than predictive since they are statements about information-distribution systems that are changing very rapidly. People may respond quite differently to the newer forms of mediated communication; it is still people, however, who constitute the social and communication networks of society. Thus we may find some constancy, some threads of similarity, in the consequences of information diffusion in social networks.

Predictive Propositions

6.1 The network of acquaintances is such that the odds are good (about 50–50) that two people can be linked by two intermediate acquaintances; this small world concept increases the likelihood that information will spread quite widely.

Some have conjectured that the disintegration of society may be linked to the development of isolated communities. That is, the less contact people have with those outside their immediate environment, the greater the likelihood that they will become at least socially isolated. The mass media have reduced the probability of certain kinds of isolation, while modern transportation systems have provided opportunities for large numbers of people to visit all parts of the country. Our industrialized society—with giant corporations transferring and moving individuals and families from one end of the country to the other—facilitates interaction among a vast number of different social groups. The network of acquaintances is expanded and isolation reduced. By coupling mass communication and mass transportation with a massive government and industrial network, we produce a society much like a large family in which any two people, no matter how physically remote from each other, are linked by a distant cousin. The more movement in society, the greater the probability that the number of intermediate linkages will be quite small. Thus Milgram (1967) pointed out that there is "only about one chance in two hundred thousand that any two Americans chosen at random will know each other. However, when you ask the chances of their having a mutual acquaintance, the odds drop sharply and quite amazingly, there is better than a 50–50 chance that any two people can be linked up with two intermediate acquaintances."

Of course, there may be barriers between people, such as ethnic background, occupation, and social standing, that create such enormous acquaintance gaps that information might conceivably never be transmitted between these groups. The mass media tend to bridge widely different groups and create a community of ideas among their members. Personal messages, however, are usually transmitted through networks of personal acquaintances. A community of feeling is generated through personal contacts that diffuse information about products, services, and reputations. From studies of small-world acquaintance networks, we have learned that, although a societal communication network may exist, its functioning may have strong implications for integrating our social system—in other words, we are potentially bound to one another by a communication system unique to this time.

Abstract

Jeffrey Travers and Stanley Milgram, "An Experimental Study of the Small World Problem," *Sociometry*, Vol. 32 (Dec. 1969), pp. 425–432.

Travers and Milgram attempted to answer this question: Did a social communication network of personal acquaintances exist that would allow a message to be transmitted from a stranger in one part of the country to a stranger in another part, using only a chain of persons who knew each other on a first name basis? An arbitrary target person and a group of starting persons were selected, and an attempt was made to generate an acquaintance chain from each starter to the target. A starting population of 296 volunteers were solicited: 196 were from Nebraska—100 of whom were chosen because they were owners of blue chip stocks—and 100 were from Boston. Also involved in the study were 453 intermediaries, but they were solicited by the other participants as acquaintances who could advance the message. Participants were not paid nor were other rewards offered as an incentive for completing the chains. The initial 296 volunteers were sent a folder that described the study, requested the recipient to become a participant, and presented a set of rules and the name of the target person (a stockholder living in Massachusetts) with selective information about him. Participants were also given a roster to which they were to affix their name (to prevent people from sending the document to someone who had already received it), and a stack of 15 business reply cards asking for information about each participant (to enable the researchers to keep a running track of the progress of each chain). Initial volunteers were instructed to mail the folder directly to the target person if they had previously met and knew each other on a first name basis. Otherwise, they were to mail it to a friend, relative, or close acquaintance, known on a first-name basis, who was more likely to know the target person.

Of the 296 volunteers, 217 actually sent the folder on to acquaintances. Sixty-four (29%) of the folders actually sent eventually reached the target. Within that group, the mean number of intermediaries between starters and the target was 5.2. Before reaching the target, 48% of the chains passed through only three persons.

■ The research on acquaintance links clearly indicates that networks of communication exist which connect the various social groups from one end of the country to the other. Such extensive linkages make it possible for messages to sweep across the country at great speeds, leading to the rapid spread of rumors as well as factual information. In a sense, we live in a communication society, where community truly represents people living in close association with one another, although they are separated physically by large distances. By means of acquaintance networks, messages may flow and bring people together in common understanding.

6.2 The diffusion of information on a wide scale occurs through the communication facilities of the mass media.

When radios, motion pictures, and television were undreamed of, information reached the bulk of the people rather slowly, if at all, primarily by word of mouth. Ballads, legends, and reports of itinerate salesmen and preachers were some of the ways in which people became informed. Now, however, initial exposure to information about events in all parts of the world comes from television and newspapers, which are seen by most adults in the economically advanced cultures of the world. Television is in nearly 95% of American homes and more than 85% of American adults regularly read newspapers. Except in rare instances, most of what we know about practically everything other than our closest surroundings comes to us through the mass media.

Research on the spread of information about special news events indicates that television and newspapers do provide exposure. Greenberg (1964a), for example, reported that the assassination of President John F. Kennedy was known by more than two out of three people within the first 15 to 30 minutes after it was made public through the media; and 95% or more were knowledgable within the first hour and a half. In addition, many who learned about the assassination from personal contacts sought out the broadcast media for further information. In a study of 18 news stories, Greenberg discovered that the mass media was listed overwhelmingly as the first means of learning about 17 of the events (Greenberg, 1964b). In summarizing the findings of approximately 35 different studies on how farm people get and accept new ideas, Beal and Bohlen (1957) indicated that when these individuals became aware of some new idea, such as hybrid seed corn, they mentioned hearing about the new idea first through the mass media more often than through any other source. In these studies, mass media included radio, television, newspapers, and farm magazines. At the interest stage, when a person wanted more information about an idea, the mass media were again mentioned as the first sources of information. The evidence seems to indicate that the mass media served an impelling function in diffusing information.

Abstract

Otto M. Larsen and Richard J. Hill, "Mass Media and Interpersonal Communication in the Diffusion of a News Event," *American Sociological Review,* Vol. 19 (Aug. 1954), pp. 426–433.

This study was designed to discover who learns the news, when, by what means, and how such knowledge affects subsequent communication behavior. On Friday, July 31, 1953, at 7:30 A.M. (Pacific Standard Time), Senator Robert A. Taft died in a New York City hospital. News of this event was flashed to all parts of the country by the media of mass communication. The first reports of Taft's death reached Seattle, Washington, from a major wire service at approximately 7:45 A.M. By 8:00 A.M., six major radio stations in the city had broadcast the news at least once. At 10:45 A.M., the first television program of the day in the Seattle area carried the story. The first newspaper report appeared on the downtown newsstands at 2:30 P.M. Twenty-four hours after the first report, a poll was conducted in a housing area occupied by University of Washington faculty members; 147 interviews were completed in an attempt to cover the entire population. Husbands and wives were interviewed separately. Interviews opened as follows: "We are studying how people learn of an important news event. Friday morning a prominent national official died. Do you know who that was?" If the answer was "Taft," he or she was asked five additional questions relevant to diffusion of the news event. Two-and-a-half days later, alternate occupied dwelling units in a low-rent adult housing project located near the industrial section of Seattle, in which 176 units were occupied, were canvassed. Interviews numbering 137 were secured, with male and female adult members of each household being interviewed independently whenever

possible. In this labor-class sample the time differential allowed for a greater memory error and opportunity in which to discuss the event with others.

The study showed that 88% of the faculty and 93% of the labor group knew of Senator Taft's death at the time of the interview. Within the faculty community, men and women knew the news in almost equal proportions, while a slightly greater proportion of the men knew the news in the labor community. In each community, 99% of the whites and 86% of the blacks knew the news. Radio was the single most important source of the news (54% of the faculty and 43% of the labor class) while 25% of the labor group and only 5% of the faculty were informed by television; 35% of the faculty and 17% of the labor group were informed by interpersonal communication. The newspaper was the source of information for 6% of the faculty and 15% of the labor group. In the labor group more females than males learned of the death from television, while males were first informed by newspapers to a greater degree than females. The faculty community heard the news considerably earlier than the labor community (10:45 A.M. vs. 4:00 P.M. as the median hour of exposure). In both communities females heard the news earlier than males. Once the news was known in both communities, similar patterns of interpersonal communication followed. With a given community, however, males talked to more people about the death than did females. Those who learned by word of mouth told more people about the news than did those who learned from the mass media.

■ Research on the diffusion of information indicates rather clearly that individuals become exposed to events of national concern more often through the mass media—radio, television, and newspapers—than through interpersonal communication. However, interpersonal contacts follow quickly thereafter. If we wish to diffuse information on a wide scale, our best choice is one of the mass media and, most likely, one of the electronic media such as radio or television.

6.3   Word-of-mouth communication informs potential buyers, circulates rumors, and operates the grapevine.

Although we have just discussed situations in which information is diffused most readily through the mass media, circumstances also exist in which word-of-mouth or interpersonal communication plays a major role. Word-of-mouth information consists of a series of individual reports of what people remember. Most research interviewers on this kind of communication have people recollect when they became aware of the information, from what source they received it, what they did in response to the information, and to whom they communicated it at a later time. Word-of-mouth communication that occurs in a formal organization (business, industry, government) but without management's official sanction is often called the *grapevine*. Sometimes such information is quite factual and other times it seems to be completely inaccurate. *Rumor* refers to word-of-mouth communication in which the information is considered generally to be false. When information about an incident is passed by word of mouth with no firm evidence or official sanction, we call the process *rumor* and the information *gossip*. When something happens that cannot be confirmed, information is often sought from members of a community or a crowd that has witnessed it. Just prior to riots, word-of-mouth information may be passed that helps explain what has happened, what is currently happening, and also what may happen. If the happening seems probable but cannot be confirmed, we say that a rumor has started. On the other hand, a person possessing information about a new product, for example, will often be eager to pass on this knowledge in a manner similar to that of the rumor process, but without the taint of false information associated with rumors. In all three forms of communication—the grapevine, the rumor, and word-of-mouth advertising—information is diffused through social groups.

Personal sources of information and the diffusion of information by word of mouth serve the function of informing buyers as well as influencing them to make purchases.

Abstract

Jagdish N. Sheth, "Word-of-Mouth In Low-Risk Innovations," *Journal of Advertising Research,* Vol. 11 (June 1971), pp. 15–18.

When considering what part word-of-mouth communication plays in making potential buyers aware of a new, popular, low-risk supermarket product, Sheth hypothesized that buyers tend not to pay much attention to the mass media advertisements because they believe the information is likely to be exaggerated and unhelpful. As a result, they rely instead on word-of-mouth information.

To test this hypothesis, more than 900 male respondents were personally interviewed in 1964 about the stainless steel razorblades just introduced on the market that year. Questions were asked about the respondents' shaving habits, their awareness of the new stainless steel blades, their adoption and continued use of them—if such was the case—and brand preferences. Finally, they were asked to recollect the time they became aware of the new blades, what source informed them for the first time, whether they used them immediately after hearing about them or sometime later, and whether friends or other personal informal sources were influential in their decision to try them. If they were users, they were also asked whether they had influenced someone else to try the new blades. Of the respondents, 601 used double-edged stainless steel blades and shaved at least two to four times a week. Data are based on that sample.

According to 36% of the respondents, a personal source accounted for their becoming aware of the razorblades; 48% stated they were also influenced by a personal source in their decision to try them. It was after their own adoption, 18% stated, that they had influenced someone else to buy some. Of the sample, 48% adopted the new blades immediately after learning about them. Seventy-one percent of the respondents were both informed and influenced by a personal source as compared with only 35% of those who were made aware by an impersonal source. As many as 25% of the respondents who admitted they were influenced by a personal source attempted to influence someone else, whereas only 9% of those not influenced by a personal source attempted to influence others.

Abstract

Keith Davis, "A Method of Studying Communication Patterns in Organizations," *Personnel Psychology,* Vol. 6 (1953), pp. 301–312.

Davis was concerned with studying the flow of information in formal organizations. He wanted to discover its sequence and rate of flow, along with what media were used. The investigator, with the assistance of company officials, selected the event or information that was the subject of each survey and made it available to selected members of the organization. After a period of time a survey questionnaire was prepared and delivered to each respondent at his or her work location. The questionnaire included six questions to be answered by respondents who knew all or part of the information. These questions were: (1) From whom did you first receive the information? (2) By what method did you first receive the information? (3) Where were you when you first received the information? (4) How long before (the date of the survey) did you first receive the information? (5) From how many sources did you receive the information? (6) Did you pass the information or part of it to another employee? If so, circle the approximate number of individuals to whom you passed the information.

Only a few persons who knew a unit of information ever passed it on—generally a person who would be considered a *liaison.* For example, with a quality-control incident, 68% of the executives received the information, but only 20% transmitted it to someone else. In general, the flow of information was relatively rapid. In one instance, the wife of a particular manager had a baby at the local hospital at 11:00 P.M., and by 2:00 P.M. the next day 46% of the entire management group knew about the event. The news was transmitted primarily by word of mouth and an occasional interoffice telephone call. Most transmission occurred immediately before work began, during a coffee break, or during the lunch hour. In this study of the grapevine in business organizations, Davis concluded that this type of word-of-mouth communication was very fast, that it was selective in that people who were *not* supposed to hear about certain information *did not get the information,* that information about the company flowing through the grapevine did so primarily at the place of work, and that the grapevine seemed to be most effective when there was an active, formal communication program.

Abstract

Warren A. Peterson and Noel P. Gist, "Rumor and Public Opinion," *American Journal of Sociology,* Vol. 57 (Sept. 1951), pp. 159–167.

After reviewing research on rumors conducted in the laboratory, which tended to show they grew shorter, became more concise, and were more easily grasped as they were spread, Peterson and Gist wanted to determine whether real rumors about an actual incident would undergo similar changes. They decided to observe and record the rumors circulating in a small midwestern city about an unsolved rape and murder of a 15-year-old girl, who was babysitting when she was attacked and killed. They asked about 100 university students residing in various parts of the city to write down any rumor or any information they had heard the previous week about the case. The statements were grouped according to topics and analyzed on the basis of earlier experimental studies of rumor—that is, information undergoes leveling (message becomes shorter and more concise), sharpening (selected details are highlighted), and assimilation (feelings and attitudes of reporters become a part of the report).

Immediately after the crime, rumors began to circulate, most of which were varied, scattered, and of short duration. It was speculated that the murderer was a black, a high school student, a cab driver, a feeble-minded boy, and even the employer of the babysitter. The most common and pivotal rumor, to which the most short-lived rumors related, was that Mr. X, the babysitter's employer, had raped and murdered the girl after leaving a party he and his wife were attending. These short-term rumors, representing a wide and detailed variety of interpretations, concerned (1) Mr. X's absence from the party, (2) the detection and arrest of Mr. X, (3) evidence concerning the attack, (4) evidence supplied by individuals, (5) reactions of Mr. X, and (6) impressions of Mr. X. Seventy-five different rumors were reported.

Of the three kinds of changes that customarily occur in laboratory rumors (leveling, sharpening, and assimilation), only sharpening seemed evident. Those who were keenly interested in the case remembered and emphasized details that made their report plausible. However, something similar to assimilation had occurred to make the pivotal speculation that Mr. X was the murderer more impressive and sensational, but the variety of rumors suggested that assimilation had failed to make reports of the incident coherent and well rounded.

■ The flow of rumors in a community, like information carried on the grapevine in a business, seems to depend both on the relationship that the topic of the rumor has to the individual and on its clarity. Ambiguous rumors may prevent the individual from obtaining complete and accurate information. Contrary to laboratory results on rumor transmission, this study discovered that an actual rumor tends to become more elaborated and diversified rather than to become shorter, more concise, and more easily grasped as it is spread.

Research on diffusing information suggests that personal sources and word-of-mouth communication inform the public and often reassures them that their decisions to adopt new ideas and products are legitimate. The research also suggests that the spread of word-of-mouth information in business organizations occurs in selective, rapid, and cluster-like chains. Key liaison individuals serve more often as transmitters of information, resulting in a degree of isolation for those who are not a part of the communication network. Individuals also tend to take information from reports in the mass media and incorporate it into their word-of-mouth representations. However, many factors influence how people will receive information about new products, ideas, events in the community, and changes in business. Yet, we are confident that word-of-mouth communication is a very important source.

6.4 The communication network—who can talk to whom—affects the efficiency of information diffusion and the morale of members of the network.

The basic characteristic of communication networks concerns who can talk to whom or who can get information from whom, or who will provide information to whom. In research on the small world concept, acquaintance networks were created in order to get information from one part of the country to another. In a community or a business organization, the grapevine and rumor networks evolve from the nature of the information being distributed. In formal organizations, like the military, the chain of command dictates who may talk to whom. In other groups, the status and prestige of certain individuals accords them the privilege of being the ones through whom everyone must go in order to get information to other people. Because of the widespread imposition of communication patterns on people, questions have been raised about what effect a fixed pattern of interaction may have on how efficiently information gets to people and how people *feel* about what the group is doing and how well it is getting done. Bavelas (1950) suggested that the pattern of communication might affect the emergence of leadership, the development of organization, the degree to which a group resists being disrupted, and the ability of the group to adapt successfully to sudden changes in the work environment. Although answers to these questions are not entirely clear or definite, evidence suggests that different communication patterns produce the following effects:

1. The individual in the most central position (the position through which others send messages) consistently emerges as the leader of the group.

2. The more central the position in the network, the more satisfied the member occupying the position will be with the work of the group.

3. Of four basic patterns studied, the highly centralized wheel appears to be the most efficient (having fewer errors and completing the task in a shorter time).

Wheel

4. The "Y" pattern is more efficient than the chain.

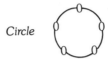

Y Pattern   0—0—0

Chain   0—0—0—0—0

5. The circle pattern is the least efficient, with participants mostly sending messages until they can work out the answer themselves.

Circle

6. The circle pattern, however, seems to produce the highest levels of satisfaction in members.

7. Highly centralized networks, such as the wheel, Y, and chain, tend to place heavy information-processing demands on the centralized positions. The result is that with complex tasks, the person in the central position becomes overloaded and the efficiency of the group decreases. Since the circle pattern is highly decentralized, the responsibilities for information processing are dispersed throughout the positions, resulting in greater efficiency with complex problems. The circle pattern seems to have greater adaptability to changes in demands for handling problems.

Where a communication pattern is not imposed on a group, evidence seems to indicate that most groups can work efficiently by evolving a pattern that meets the demands of its members and the task to be completed. Burgess (1968) demonstrated that the wheel and the circle patterns ultimately develop operating procedures that make them equally efficient. Differences began to wash out only after approximately 900 problems had been solved, however, and participants had evolved a satisfactory working relationship. Nevertheless, with short-term groups in which structural demands are placed on interaction, the pattern of communication may seriously affect participants' satisfaction and efficiency.

Abstract

Harold J. Leavitt, "Some Effects of Certain Communication Patterns on Group Performance," *Journal of Abnormal and Social Psychology*, Vol. 46 (1951), pp. 38–50.

Leavitt was concerned with how different communication patterns would affect the results in the performance of group tasks. He selected 100 male undergraduates and split them into 20 groups of 5 men each. These 20 groups were divided so that 5 groups were tested on each of the 4 experimental patterns. The communication patterns used were the circle, chain, Y, and wheel. Each group was given 15 consecutive trials on one pattern, a process requiring one session of about 50 minutes. The order in which the patterns were used was randomized, and positions were shifted for each new group to reduce the effect of geographical position. After a group had completed 15 trials, and before members were permitted to talk with one another, each person filled out a questionnaire. The task to be completed by each group was to discover the single, common symbol from among several symbols. Each subject was given a card, labeled by color, on which there was a set of five out of a possible six symbols. Each subject's card was different from all the others in that the missing symbol was different in each case. Thus, in any set of five cards there was only one symbol in common. The task was for every member to find the common symbol. To accomplish this, each member was allowed to write to those people in the group to whom he had an open channel, a link in the diagrammed patterns. Every separate written message from one subject to another was considered one communication. Any subject who discovered the answer was allowed to pass it along. When all five indicated they knew the common symbol, the trial was ended.

The wheel operated in the same way in all five cases. The organization that evolved by the fifth trial and used in the balance of the 15 trials was having the peripheral men funnel information to the center, where a decision was made and sent out. The Y operated so that the most central position was given complete decision-making authority. The next most central position served only as a transmitter of information. In the chain, information was usually funneled in from both ends and sent out in both directions. The circle showed no consistent operational organization. Most commonly, messages were just sent in both directions until any subject received an answer or worked one out. All available links were used at some time during the course of each trial. A measure in terms of seconds to complete a trial indicated that the fastest single trial for the wheel was considerably faster than the fastest single trial for the circle. The circle pattern also clearly used more messages to solve a problem than any other pattern; it also made more errors than any of the others but corrected a greater proportion of them.

■ The ways in which people are linked to one another in communication networks may in itself influence the manner in which they get information. The restriction of information flow to a particular pattern may produce more final errors, shorten the time necessary to solve a problem, encourage strong centralized leadership, or increase or reduce morale or satisfaction with group operations. Selecting the network most suited to the task we want to accomplish is an important part of effectively communicating in social groups.

Summary

Communication is essential for the efficient functioning of social groups. Whenever tasks must involve a group rather than a single individual, the diffusion of information among the members of the group is one of the essential processes. In our society we have developed a wide variety of means for diffusing information through many different networks. Although we may exist physically isolated from many members of society, the network of acquaintances we have evolved makes it likely that we can link ourselves with other people, and increase the possibility of spreading information rapidly. Of course, the development of extensive facilities for mass media makes diffusing information on a national or international scale almost immediate. In most developed or developing countries, this information is rapidly spread to individuals. In addition to the mass media, the flow of word-of-mouth information through the grapevine, by rumor, or word-of-mouth advertising provides a means of diffusing information among individuals. Such word-of-mouth communication is usually very fast and rather influential. A variety of communication networks exists, each influencing the efficiency of information diffusion and the morale of those who are members of a network. Understanding the flow of information in groups is important to understanding effective group interaction.

Background Readings

The literature on social groups is itself diffused among the publications of such diverse fields as rural sociology and speech communication. Information diffusion through social groups is part of rumor, propaganda, advertising, and community problems. These readings provide a general introduction to the breadth and depth to which this topic can lead a person.

Katz, Daniel, and Robert L. Kahn, *The Social Psychology of Organizations* (New York: John Wiley & Sons, 1966). Chapter 9, "Communication: The Flow of Information," examines social systems as restricted communication networks. An excellent theoretical explanation.

Miller, George A., *Language and Communication: A Scientific and Psychological Introduction* (New York: McGraw-Hill Book Co., 1951). Chapter 12, "The Social Approach," is a concise but early statement on research relating small group networks, rumors, and diffusion studies to a central theme.

Pool, Ithiel de Sola, Wilbur Schramm, Frederick W. Frey, Nathan Maccoby, and Edwin B. Parker, eds., *Handbook of Communication* (Chicago: Rand-McNally & Co., 1973). Chapter 1, "Communication Systems," and Chapter 11, "Mass Media and Interpersonal Communication" represent the most current summary and synthesis available of studies on information flow and diffusion in organizations, small groups, large networks such as regions, communities, and nations.

7.1 The importance of a message, to whom it is important, the medium used in its reproduction, and the number of people who have already heard it determine the speed and direction in which it is reproduced.

7.2 If information is reproduced serially, details of the message will likely become omitted (leveling), added (adding), highlighted (sharpening), and/or modified to conform to the interest needs and feelings of the reproducers (assimilating.)

7.3 If appropriate correctives are applied in serial communication, distortions can be reduced.

7.4 A knowledge of the personal characteristics of the communicators helps to predict the kind of distortion that will result from serial communication.

Chapter 7
Serial Groups

If the two person dyad or unit is expanded so a message is relayed from Person A to Person B to Person C to Person D to Person E by a series of two person interactions in which each individual interprets and then transmits a message to the next person in the chain, we call this *serial communication* or the *serial reproduction of information*. This latter term comes from the work of the psychologist Sir Frederic Bartlett (1932), who believed that this was a satisfactory system for memory experiments. Since his research, the method of serial reproduction has been used to study the patterns and effects both of rumors in many localities and of grapevines in various organizations. Serial communication is an often neglected but vital communication system. In a highly structured organization or society, the information that can be gleaned from the grapevine is generally considered to have greater value (judging from the reactions of receivers) than most official announcements. Because of its convenience and interest, serial communication is used extensively. Much of the information diffused throughout the community or organization is carried through such communication, the nature of the network involved largely determining its success. In addition, the serial nature of this communication system itself affects the success of messages. This latter variable will be our concern in this chapter.

This chapter is based on material originally prepared by Timothy B. Hegstrom of West Valley College, Saratoga, California.

Predictive Propositions

7.1 The importance of a message, to whom it is important, the medium used in its reproduction, and the number of people who have already heard it determine the speed and direction in which it is reproduced.

While the phenomenon of serial reproduction is present in many social situations, the speed with which a message is passed varies greatly, as does the number of people to whom it is passed. In many situations, a rumor spreads rapidly from one person to another till almost everyone has heard some version. In other situations, very few people hear the rumor. The probability that a message will be passed on to additional receivers is greatest when about half the population has heard it (Dodd, 1953, 1958). It will also travel furthest and fastest at that time. Other factors that seem to determine whether a rumor will be passed on are the initial ambiguity of the message, since ambiguous messages tend to be repeated and distorted, and the critical faculty of those listening to it, since listeners with a high critical faculty are not as likely to pass on rumors, particularly if they seem improbable (Chorus, 1953; Buckner, 1965). In addition, the channel or method by which a message is transmitted will affect the speed of its transmission. Generally speaking, the easiest channels to use will result in the furthest and fastest spread of information. Thus, most serial reproduction in actual circumstances occurs face to face, a medium that tends to spread information the fastest (Davis, 1953).

The networks through which information is serially communicated seem to be universally interconnected and, indeed, seem to tie everyone in the world together in some way or other. This was rather clearly illustrated in the so-called "Small World Problem" discussed in Chapter 6 (Proposition 6.1).

Interestingly, it has been demonstrated that only 10% of the individuals in a business or governmental organization who receive information through the grapevine pass it on. In certain organizations that 10% involves the same people in nearly all messages (Sutton and Porter, 1968). However, some studies indicate that the liaison people vary with each message, although the percentage of those who pass information on seems to stay at around 10%.

Abstract

Leon Festinger, Stanley Schachter, and Kurt Back, *Social Pressure in Informal Groups: A Study of a Housing Project* (New York: Harper & Row, 1950), pp. 113–141.

This study on communication in a social group was concerned with determining what factors would affect the content of a message, to whom it is communicated, and its acceptance. In a field experiment rumors were planted in a housing project. In the two housing courts—one with favorable and the other with unfavorable attitudes toward the tenant organization or council—a rumor was independently planted that there was going to be a mass media coverage of the functioning of the tenant council. Messages were charted and analyzed using postrumor interviews and participant-observer reports.

The story planted in the court with the unconcerned attitude spread to very few people, while that planted in the other court spread significantly further. The persons who were interested and involved were more likely to receive, spread, and be affected by the content of the rumor.

■ It appears that those individuals who are interested or are likely to be affected by the subject of a rumor are more likely to be involved in communicating the message. The more important the message is to them the more likely it is that it will be serially reproduced. In addition, information will travel more rapidly to individuals who may find it relevant. Thus when we desire to diffuse information through serial communication, there is an obvious advantage in telling those who are most likely to transmit the information to others through the easiest possible channel. This probably means that information should be given initially to individuals concerned with the subject and that such information should usually be transmitted through face-to-face oral communication. As a rule, we can expect information in which people have little interest to fail to be reproduced very widely. Such information dies on the vine.

7.2   If information is reproduced serially, details of the message will likely become omitted (leveling), added (adding), highlighted (sharpening), and/or modified to conform to the interest needs and feelings of the reproducers (assimilating).

In serial communication it is difficult to maintain the accuracy of the original message as it is passed from one person to another. Among the variety of errors likely to occur are *leveling, adding, sharpening,* and *assimilating.* When a message is *leveled,* it means that an individual omits several details when he tells it to the next person in the chain. This may be out of a desire to simplify the message or it may simply occur because of the limitations of human memory. Leveling is probably one of the most common characteristics of serial communication. The *adding* of ideas that spring full blown from the minds of the communicators can also change the initial message. Both leveling and adding are the building blocks for other kinds of error.

Distortions of the original material may occur through *sharpening* and *assimilating. Sharpening* occurs when the central theme of a rumor is accepted as true and the communicator reorganizes and distorts the details of the message to make them consistent with that theme. Sometimes he or she also adds materials. The error of *assimilating* refers to the tendency to change messages into more personally satisfying forms so they are more congenial either to the source or the receiver. For example, in a conversation between a business manager and his subordinate, the latter might modify his message to make it conform to the biases of his supervisor or to make it more acceptable or painless to himself. Individuals tend to perceive selected aspects of their environment and to filter these perceptions through past experiences, moods, attitudes, and emotional states. Such filtering results in a compromise between the original message and the cognitive and affective state of the reproducer of the message.

In his research on serial communication, Brissey (1964) collected data on two types of error as he determined a subject's completion ratio (the complement of an error of omission) and discrimination ratio (the complement of an error of addition). His study required that the subject complete a task at each link in the serial reproduction chain. The task was described in the message he was asked to reproduce. Brissey's conclusion was that the process of serial reproduction results in a distortion in both task performance and message reproduction. Some question arises as to whether findings in laboratory experiments on serial reproduction are applicable to real life situations or to the grapevine in organizations. Allport and Postman (1947) indicated that their experience with wartime rumor clinics showed that most of the same distortion patterns characteristic of serial reproduction experiments were equally true in the field situation. However, others who have analyzed the research disagree. The majority of field studies on rumor do not obtain as large a degree of distortion as the laboratory studies. The explanation may be that in the laboratory the subject is required to reproduce the message, whereas in real life he may not feel any pressure to repeat material of which he himself is unsure. Also, if he hears a message several times through an actual grapevine, he has a greater opportunity to check for error before passing it on. In addition, he may have had some experience with the material in the message and thus be able to judge its plausibility. If it is implausible, he may change it in such a way that when he passes it on, he will make it more accurate than the original message—in other words, the "return-to-truth" phenomenon occurs. Also, in real life the communicator can ask to have the message repeated as many times as necessary.

Abstract

Gordon Allport and Leo Postman, *The Psychology of Rumor* (New York: Holt, Rinehart and Winston, 1947).

This experiment, conducted in classrooms before student audiences and, more privately, in laboratories, was an attempt to determine the variety of ways in which information became distorted in a rumor situation. Six or seven subjects were called individually into a classroom or laboratory to hear and then repeat a message. A "busy picture" on a slide was projected onto a screen so that the first subject could observe and describe at least 20 details of the photo to a second person from whom the screen was concealed. A third subject entered the room and, after hearing the description of the picture from the second person, passed it on to the fourth, and so on. Allport and Postman recorded the messages, or descriptions, for future analysis.

Their analysis indicated distortion in rumor through leveling, sharpening, and assimilating. By the fifth or sixth time the description was passed on, approximately 70% of the original details had been leveled from the message. Most leveling, Allport and Postman found, occurred at the beginning of the serial reproduction chain. As the message passed through the chain, it was eventually leveled to a sentence or two, at which point the information was passed on mainly through memory. Leveling did not result in the total elimination of the information. Sharpening was evident in the rationalizing of unfamiliar message data so that, by fitting a central theme, it was more meaningful to the recipient. Individuals often introduced closure into messages by completing descriptions even though the reproduction they heard was somewhat incomplete. Sometimes individuals would remember odd words or phrases better than routine wordings—"twit the twerp" might be recalled just because it is odd or stands out. Some changes in the reproduced messages were due to a recipient's intellectual and emotional state of mind—attributable to the process of assimilation.

■ From this study the effective communicator should realize that if information is serially reproduced, details will be omitted or added, and both sharpening and assimilating will occur. The underlying causes for error in serial communication are, of course, similar to those in any dyad since serial communication is but an extension of this two-way exchange. In fact, an increase in the number of communication encounters compounds the problems of perception and description typically found in a dyad. A detailed message passed by word of mouth through a serial chain will probably become distorted in the ways suggested above. An awareness of the possibility of such errors makes it essential for the source of the message to find the means for preventing distortions and for the receiver to help reduce information loss by his efforts.

7.3   If appropriate correctives are applied in serial communication, distortions can be reduced.

The problems of distortion just discussed seem to be a persistent drawback in serial communication. However, these distortions are not inevitable, since rumors sometimes pass with a high degree of accuracy to a large number of people. To reduce the chance of error considerably, there are possible correctives. Pace and Boren (1973, pp. 356) suggested a number of such correctives that might help the individuals involved in a serial communication chain. Unfortunately, most of them have not been tested experimentally in a serial communication situation; however, they do seem helpful to those who have utilized them on a personal basis. They include:

1.   Giving details in an appropriate order

2.   Asking the interpreter to take notes as an aid to memory and as a means of focusing his or her attention on the message

3.   Utilizing perception checking responses to determine correspondence of the meaning

4.   Using forms of emphasis to highlight points believed to be important

5.   Differentiating between empirical data and statements not based on observations to reduce the number of inaccurate inferences that may lead to misunderstanding or disbelief

6.   Interacting sensitively with the person with whom you are talking so as to avoid moving from point to point either too quickly or too slowly

7.   Presenting information in smaller and simpler units so as to reduce omissions and alterations, since the complex materials are usually shortened and simplified by the interpreter before he or she tries to communicate them to others

8.   Using previews, internal summaries, reviews, and overviews as indicators of where you are "located" in the maze of messages required to "get across" important information to others

9.   Following up a message with a summary in a different medium and form (For instance, if your message is presented in spoken form, follow it up with a written memo)

10.   Reducing the number of reproductions of a message to a minimum to avoid creating an overload, which in turn, may produce a bottleneck or a jam-up (A strategic analysis of who should get messages from whom may provide useful information about areas where network adjustments may facilitate message flow.)

Abstract

Forrest L. Brissey, "The Factor of Relevance in the Serial Reproduction of Information," *Journal of Communication,* Vol. 11 (1961), pp. 211–219.

Brissey wanted to discover possible correctives for reducing distortions in the serial reproduction of information. This study focused particularly on the question of whether the creation of a relevant set (mental set to *expect* to hear or observe certain kinds of details) would allow the retention of important details to remain fairly constant from one individual to the next.

In the experiment 180 student subjects were divided into five groups, representing five links in each chain, and asked to view a movie titled "Hit-and-Run Drivers." Unlike previous serial reproduction experiments, here each group was given a relevant mental set in the form of a common list of instructions on writing a report on the movie's content, including the methods used to apprehend the guilty person. Those in Group 1 represented the first level of the chain: eyewitness observers who were the only ones to see the film. Then each person in this group wrote a report on the methods used in apprehending the hit-and-run driver. Group 2 subjects, the second link in the chain, were randomly assigned reports from Group 1. Each person in this group read the report once, then wrote his or her account of it before passing it on to the members of Group 3—and so on through Groups 4 and 5. After writing their reports, members of each group were given a true or false posttest. An analysis of their answers indicated whether they were informed, misinformed, or uninformed (and to what degree) with regard to the information presented in the film.

There were definite differences in the reports given by the various links in the chain, the tendency being to lose relevant information from one person to the next. Each group, however, tended to be more informed than misinformed. The mean relevance values of the information found in Groups 2 through 5 were nearly equal. Even though information was lost through the serial reproduction chains, what was retained was the most relevant information presented. The fact that distortion in this experiment seems to be less than that in previous experiments in serial communication indicates that the creation of a common relevant set for all links in the chain can reduce the amount.

■ Apparently there are some correctives that, when applied, will reduce the distortion commonly occurring in serial reproduced messages. One technique that might help reduce information loss in serial reproduction is to provide cues to assist a communicator to focus on key or relevant ideas so they will be retained in successive reproductions. Perhaps, the other suggestions listed above would have a comparably beneficial effect on reducing distortion in serial reproduced messages.

7.4 A knowledge of the personal characteristics of the communicators helps to predict the kind of distortion that will result from serial communication.

Levitt (1952) came to the conclusion that "some unknown characteristic or characteristics of the individual played a part in determining whether that individual would be rumor-prone or rumor-resistant." He discovered that some individuals are likely to distort a great deal of the information transmitted to them while others are less likely to do so. If we could know the individual characteristics of the communicators, we might be able to predict with what accuracy a message would be reproduced. It is only a small step from the concept of *assimilation* (individuals distort because of differences in their needs, attitudes, experiences, etc.) to the conclusion that understanding an individual will give information about the way in which a message will be altered. For example, in a serial reproduction experiment, Johnson and Wood (1944) found that subjects who extremely liked or disliked blacks as measured by an attitude survey were more likely to include such information in their message reproductions that conformed to their known prejudices. In the group with an unfavorable attitude toward blacks, a significantly greater number of unfavorable message units were retained the third time they were reproduced than in the group favorable toward blacks.

There are also differences in the ways that communicators tend to remember messages. Leveling and sharpening have been suggested as being at opposite poles in a continuum of memory organization. Holzman and his colleagues (Holzman and Gardner, 1959; Gardner and Lohrenz, 1960; Holzman and Gardner, 1960) have developed a "Schematizing Test" to distinguish levelers from sharpeners. The levelers seem also to be assimilators, and thus distort information to fit their memory of past experience and attitudes. The sharpeners, by contrast, are less likely to assimilate.

Abstract

Riley W. Gardner and Leander J. Lohrenz, "Leveling–Sharpening and Serial Reproduction of a Story," *Bulletin of the Menninger Clinic*, Vol. 24 (1960), pp. 295–304.

Gardner and Lohrenz attempted to discover whether a story would be transmitted differently through a serial reproduction chain of levelers than it would be through a chain of sharpeners—particularly with regard to the amount of leveling, distortion, and addition. A "Schematizing Test" was given to 30 subjects and, based on the results, five women levelers and five women sharpeners were chosen to form chains for a serial reproduction exercise. Six months later, a story, "The Son Who Tried to Outwit His Father," was reproduced orally through the chain of levelers and, in another session, through the chain of sharpeners. There was a two-minute lapse between hearing and telling the story, during which time subjects left the room if they had finished telling the story or entered the room if they were about to hear it.

Both groups showed changes as the message was reproduced. However, the levelers produced more omissions, distortions, and additions in their reproductions than those classified as sharpeners. In this particular experiment, measurable characteristics of the communicators made it possible to predict the kind and extent of distortion that would occur.

■ Individuals who can be classified as levelers will omit, distort, and add more new information than individuals who are sharpeners. Some communication responsibilities may require the attention of a sharpener rather than a leveler because of the importance of accurately transmitting information. In all likelihood there are a number of other personal characteristics that influence the manner in which an individual reproduces messages in a serial chain. Efforts to discover these characteristics would be particularly useful in improving the accuracy of such messages.

Summary

In many organizations and in society at large, information is largely transmitted through serial communication. The importance and relevance of the message to its recipient will influence the speed and direction in which the information is reproduced. The number of people who have already heard the message and the medium used to reproduce it will result in the further and faster spread of information. Serial communication is also likely to result in important changes in the details of the message; however, correctives can be used to reduce these changes. An understanding of the personal characteristics of the individuals involved in a serial chain would probably help us predict the kinds of changes most likely to occur.

Background Readings

Most of the data we have on the serial reproduction of information in communication networks is derived from experiments in laboratories and from anecdotes concerning how misunderstandings occur when you try to get a message from person to person to person in an organization or a neighborhood. These selections bring together research on serial reproduction and present the clearest picture available.

Barnlund, Dean C., *Interpersonal Communication: Survey and Studies* (Boston: Houghton Mifflin Co., 1968). The section on "Channels of Communication: Serial Transmission" summarizes selected but classic research on serial communication into a compact unit.

Peterson, Brent D., Gerald M. Goldhaber, and R. Wayne Pace, *Communication Probes* (Palo Alto, Calif.: Science Research Associates, 1974). The section on "Serial Relationships" is the most complete treatment of serial communication in an introductory communication textbook. Presented in an entertaining manner, this text-reader offers the expertise of various specialists in the field.

Redding, W. Charles, *Communication within the Organization: An Interpretive Review of Theory and Research* (New York: Industrial Communication Council, 1972). In a section on "Serial Transmission Effect," the author lists serial transmission effect as the ninth fundamental postulate of communication in human organizations. Serial communication is explained in direct and understandable terms.

Part 4
Achieving Change

As communicators we often speak or interact with others to influence or change their behavior. What is involved in persuading an individual to change his or her behavior? What steps or techniques can we use to achieve behavioral change? This section will consider propositions that deal with some possible answers to these questions. The roles of individuals, small groups, and society will be discussed according to the effects they each have on persuading or achieving behavioral change in people.

Achieving change or persuading others is an art that has been studied and practiced for thousands of years. The scientific approach to enhancing persuasion, however, is new to this century. This section will look at some of the new-found evidence and will consider how the persuader may use this information to become more effective in achieving change. The propositions and the studies included in this section are the outcomes, largely, of scientific methodology. However, an uncritical acceptance of the contents of this section is hardly our goal. In the areas of behavioral change and persuasion, science is not so advanced as to preclude modification or even complete dismissal of any or all of our present research findings. We hope you will critically analyze, replicate, change, and extend the findings presented here.

Karlins and Abelson (1970) describe the present state of research in behavior and attitude change thus: "As research in persuasion continues, it becomes increasingly evident that simple, 'principles of persuasion' are the exception rather than the rule. We are beginning to appreciate the complexity of the persuasive process and realize that whether or not a person is persuaded often depends on a multiplicity of interacting factors (some still unknown). In moving from the undifferentiated to the more refined principles of persuasion, one is moving closer to an effective science of behavior control" (p. 3).

The place of the individual as an agent of change through the persuasive process is considered in Chapter 8. Chapter 9 examines the role the small group plays in bringing about behavioral change. The concluding chapter of the section, Chapter

10, deals with propositions about the processes by which social change occurs. The scientific findings and propositions discussed here should be viewed as guidelines, not as rigid boundaries in understanding behavioral change. If we approach the section with this in mind, we should gain a fuller appreciation for the persuasive process. We may, also, be able to become more effective practitioners of the art of persuasion.

8.1 If the source of a message is viewed as having high credibility, he or she will tend to achieve more attitude change.

8.2 Perceived disorganization and nonfluencies tend to reduce a speaker's credibility.

8.3 A speaker of low credibility can become more effective by arguing against his or her own best interests or by being identified after rather than before speaking.

8.4 Being tall does not seem automatically to enhance a speaker's credibility.

8.5 Being male does seem to naturally enhance a speaker's credibility.

8.6 If an individual is perceived as attractive to the person being persuaded, he or she will tend to bring about a greater change in attitude.

Chapter 8
Individual Factors

Persuasion has been defined as a communication process in which a person attempts to exert control over behavioral changes through the use of symbols (Simons, 1971; Bettinghaus, 1973, p. 10). The primary focus of persuasion is to change behavior by modifying attitudes. An attitude is commonly held to be a predisposition to respond favorably or unfavorably toward something (Simons, p. 230). Bandura (1969) indicates that functionally, as far as behavioral change is concerned, symbolic activities are part of the broad category of human responses called *awareness*. If individuals are to change their behavior, they must first be cognizant, or aware, of the stimuli designed to influence them. This statement naturally raises the question of the role in behavioral change of stimuli that are too weak or too brief to produce full recognition—sometimes called subliminal messages. After reviewing the research on this issue, Bandura observes that ". . . it would appear from the elusive and scanty yield of research in this area that subliminal activation must play a relatively inconsequential role in regulating human behavior. Whereas recognizable stimuli assume a powerful behavior-directing function, nonrecognized stimuli have, at best, weak, inconsistent, and fragmentary psychological effects" (p. 594). Smith (1973) attempted to induce conditioning under conditions of nonawareness. He was unable, however, to produce conditioning without awareness of the stimulus. Thus, we should proceed from the viewpoint that to influence behavior change effectively, messages and other stimuli must occur at the level of awareness.

Although the ultimate objective of any persuasive attempt is to change the way people behave, change agents, or persuaders, seek to modify attitudes because, for practical and other reasons, the desired behavior cannot be directly produced and reinforced. Since attitudes appear to be critical determinants of human behavior, any changes produced in them will likely influence subsequent overt responses. In addition, with the support of internal attitudes, changes in behavior will tend to be more stable and persist over a longer period of time. In other words, if you agree with a particular point of view and are inclined to support it, you will be more likely to behave as asked than if you lack a favorable attitude. Thus, developing desirable attitudes is an important concern of those who want to change behavior patterns.

Obviously, persuasion and attitude change are complex processes beset with numerous obstacles, confounding those who try to understand and thwarting those who try to bring about change. In this chapter we will examine research on factors that contribute to changes in attitudes and behavior, focusing primarily on those factors associated with the influence of individual persuaders rather than of groups or social forces. The propositions in this chapter relate primarily to the communicator and the communicatee, the persuader and the persuadee.

Predictive Propositions

8.1   If the source of a message is viewed as having high credibility, he or she will tend to achieve more attitude change.

Credibility refers to what others think of the source of a message. We are concerned particularly with individual human sources, such as a speaker who communicates directly to an audience or another individual and presents his or her own appeals for change. Although communicologists do not completely agree as to what factors contribute to high credibility, most research seems to suggest that *expertise* (perceived knowledge of the facts), *trustworthiness* (perceived integrity and lack of persuasive intent), *dynamism* (perceived enthusiasm and confidence with an acceptable degree of boldness), and *prestige* (reputation, respect, status, and popularity) are relevant and contribute both quantitatively and qualitatively to an individual's credibility. Given two individuals, one of whom is not only popular and dynamic but is also perceived as a trustworthy expert and the other who is perceived as incompetent, unreliable, dishonest, unpopular, and indecisive, the former will usually be able to influence changes in attitudes to a larger degree than the latter.

The influence of a speaker's perceived expertise and/or prestige has been tested by a number of individuals. Haiman (1949) discovered that sources who were rated as significantly more competent were also significantly more effective in changing attitudes than were other speakers.

The question of trustworthiness has also been investigated. Hovland and Weiss (1951) explored the effects of credibility by varying the trustworthiness of sources. The results of their study indicated that "initially, the information attributed to the untrustworthy sources was discounted by the subjects and had little effect on opinion change, while information attributed to trustworthy sources did achieve a significant amount of opinion change. However, data gathered after four weeks indicated that the initial differences between the trustworthy source and the untrustworthy source seemed to disappear."

Abstract

Elliot R. Siegel, Gerald R. Miller, and C. Edward Wotring, "Source Credibility and Credibility Proneness: A New Relationship," *Speech Monographs*, Vol. 36 (June 1969), pp. 118–125.

This study was an attempt to explore the relationship between credibility, attitude change, and perceived differences between the most and least acceptable sources. Knowing that some individuals perceive greater differences between message sources than do others, the authors attempted to discover whether a message presented by a highly credible source to individuals who perceived great differences between their most and least acceptable sources (low assumed similarity between opposites) would result in a greater attitude change than the same message presented to receivers who perceived little difference between their most and least acceptable sources (high assumed similarity between opposites). Conversely, they also attempted to discover the effect of a message presented by a low-credibility source to each of these groups.

Subjects, 156 undergraduate students in speech classes, who were told they were taking part in a student-opinion survey, were administered the Fiedler Assumed Similarity Between Opposites (ASO) Scale, a pretest attitude measure, and source-credibility ratings on preselected issues and sources. After 11 individuals failed to complete all parts, the other 145 students were stratified into two levels based on their ASO scores, and within each level they were assigned to one of two sources—highly credible and less credible—or to a control group. Approximately three weeks after the initial phase of data collection, an experimental message, a written argument advocating that the United States should withdraw from the United Nations, was presented to subjects in both treatment groups. A second, irrelevant message of the same length was presented to the control group. Posttest questionnaires designed to assess the perceived quality of the message—in terms of logic of arguments, amount and quality of actual data, clarity and overall quality of the message—were administered.

The ASO scale revealed that some subjects perceived great differences between their most and least acceptable sources while others perceived little difference. The low ASO subjects also perceived significantly greater differences between the high- and low-credibility sources than did the high ASO subjects. The mean attitude change for low ASO subjects exposed to the highly credible source was significantly greater than for the control group. The high ASO subjects did not change significantly in either source conditions, suggesting that they were relatively uninfluenced by such differences. When the message was linked to the highly credible source, it was rated significantly more favorable by the low ASO receivers.

■ Apparently, credibility is an important factor in influencing attitude change. Individuals viewed as being recognized experts who are trustworthy and dynamic are more likely to be successful persuaders than those lacking these qualities. However, the extent of the influence varies from individual to individual. High-prestige sources are much more persuasive with receivers who perceive significant differences between their high and low prestige sources. Some individuals are less affected by the source of a message than others. A receiver's perceptions may be a critical factor in changes that occur in response to credible sources. Instead of saying that a highly credible source will be more effective than a less credible source, what we should say, perhaps, is that subjects perceiving large differences between their most acceptable and least acceptable sources will be persuaded more by highly credible sources. In any communication situation, the source of a message carries a higher or lower degree of credibility. Research on this issue tends to support the classical claim that ethos may be the most important factor in achieving change.

8.2 Perceived disorganization and nonfluencies tend to reduce a speaker's credibility.

As suggested above, credibility is primarily a function of the perceptions of individuals who hear the speaker. Some investigators have attempted to determine the effect of the manner of presentation upon the speaker's credibility. The experimental evidence on the impact an organized or disorganized message makes seems to be somewhat contradictory. Sharp and McClung (1966) discovered that students in a classroom situation who were exposed to a disorganized speech thought less of the speaker after hearing the talk than before. On the other hand, an organized speech produced little shift in attitudes toward the speaker. This research would indicate that disorganization distracts from the speaker's credibility while organization does not necessarily contribute to credibility. Baker (1965), however, reported a significant increase in speaker credibility in the absence of disorganization cues but no significant change in credibility when disorganization was apparent. This research seems to indicate that organization contributes to credibility but disorganization makes no difference. But, for the most part, studies seem to show that organization can enhance and disorganization distract from a speaker's credibility.

Other investigations have focused on the vocal aspects of a speaker's presentation. Miller and Hewgill (1964) studied the effect of repetitions and vocalized pauses on ratings of credibility. As the number of nonfluencies increased, audience ratings of source credibility decreased. This effect was more pronounced when the nonfluent behavior involved repetitions rather than vocalized pauses. However, few significant differences resulted from audience ratings on trustworthiness. Seemingly, trustworthiness and nonfluency were not viewed as directly related. For example, an audience might rate a stutterer as trustworthy but less competent in speaking. Sereno and Hawkins (1967) also were concerned about the effect of nonfluencies on shifts in attitude and credibility. They found attitude shifts occurring in all four conditions included in the study. Apparently, varying numbers of nonfluencies did not diminish the persuasive effect of the speech. However, ratings of speaker competence and dynamism became progressively less favorable as the number of nonfluencies increased. Ratings of speaker trustworthiness did not seem to be affected by the nonfluencies.

Abstract

James C. McCroskey and R. Samuel Mehrley, "The Effects of Disorganization and Nonfluency on Attitude Change and Source Credibility," *Speech Monographs,* Vol. 36 (March 1969), pp. 13–21.

McCroskey and Mehrley attempted to discover whether serious disorganization and extensive nonfluencies would seriously restrict the amount of attitude change a communicator could effect while also substantially reducing his or her credibility.

Subjects, 352 students enrolled in a beginning public speaking course, were pretested for attitudes toward a guaranteed annual wage along with other concepts. Source credibility, as perceived by the subjects, was manipulated by a brief sketch—included in the pretest booklet—introducing each speaker. Immediately after reading these introductions, pretests for three dimensions of credibility—authoritativeness, character, and dynamism—were administered. The organized and disorganized taped speeches were ones that had been employed in earlier research on the effects of organization. Fluency or nonfluency was manipulated through the use of vocalized pauses and repetitions, which were included in the nonfluent versions in an alternating order, with a vocalized pause followed by a repetition. The nonfluent versions included 50 pauses and 50 repetitions. After hearing one of the versions of the speech, subjects were immediately asked to complete the posttest for attitude, credibility, and speech evaluation.

The introductions appear to have created the proper expectations in credibility, both low and high, but primarily in respect to authoritativeness. Analysis of posttests indicated that the highly credible source produced a more favorable change in attitude than did the one low in credibility. The well-organized, fluently presented message effected significantly more change in attitude than in any other category. The source giving the organized version of the speech was perceived as more authoritative than the one giving the disorganized version. The source presenting the fluent version of the speech was perceived as more credible than the one presenting the nonfluent version.

■ Apparently, serious disorganization and rather extensive nonfluencies, such as vocalized pauses and repetitious statements, can have a detrimental effect on the degree that attitude changes, as well as reducing the speaker's credibility. Most likely, these factors are interrelated. In addition, appropriate organization and fluent delivery seemingly increase the credibility and attitude change a speaker can achieve. In those situations where we hope to be most persuasive, we should be sure that our messages are clearly organized and delivered in a fluent manner.

8.3 A speaker of low credibility can become more effective by arguing against his or her own best interests or by being identified after rather than before speaking.

Obviously, not everyone with a worthy cause and sound arguments will be considered as highly credible. More often than we may like, the responsibility for bringing about change rests with individuals considered low in credibility. If we had to wait, however, for highly credible people to speak for us, no doubt less change than we might like would occur. This leads us to look at the conditions under which the effectiveness of low-credibility speakers can be improved. Some research has indicated that with the passage of time, the initial differences between the measured effectiveness of highly credible sources and those of low credibility tend to wash out. A "sleeper effect" occurs in which the effect of the highly credible persuader tends to wear off with time, and the effect of the speaker with low credibility tends to increase. Thus, even though you may start off with low credibility, with time, if your arguments are strong, you may be as effective as a highly credible speaker. Unfortunately, we do not always have time to wait for the "sleeper effect." Walster, Aronson, and Abrahams (1966) suggest that a low-prestige speaker can be extremely effective—perhaps even more effective than a high-prestige speaker—when arguing against his or her own self-interest. If we are able, then, to present arguments seemingly contrary to our previously established convictions, the likelihood increases that we will be more persuasive. Positions that are incongruous with the speaker's best interests (opposed to a known ideological position) appear to be the more effective with an audience. In other words, if we appear to have something to lose personally by arguing for the position we are supporting, others will more likely be persuaded to accept that position.

There is some indication that linking a message to a source with low credibility may be one of those conditions that help make individuals more resistant to change. This, apparently, is true at least when the linkage occurs prior to presenting a message. However, delaying the identification of the person until after his or her message has been presented can be a means of overcoming the negative effect of such low credibility.

Abstract

Bradley S. Greenberg and Gerald R. Miller, "The Effects of Low-Credible Sources on Message Acceptance—Experiment II: The Effect of Immediate versus Delayed Identification of a Low-Credible Source," *Speech Monographs*, Vol. 33 (June 1966), pp. 131–132.

Greenberg and Miller were interested in the effect of delaying identification of a low-credibility source until after the presentation of the message, so they could determine whether its effect would be enhanced by such a delay. In the study 71 undergraduates enrolled in speech courses were told that a project was being conducted to test their aptitude in the field of medical health. They were randomly assigned to two treatments, one in which a low-credibility source was identified immediately before the message was presented and another one in which the source was identified immediately afterwards. The message dealt with the possible health hazards of constant tooth brushing. Three items were used to assess each subject's attitude toward the topic of the message: categories ranged from "definitely disagree" to "definitely agree," with 15 scale units between the extremes.

The message source was also rated on a 7-point scale, ranging from "very good" to "very bad."

The results indicated that significantly more favorable attitudes toward the topic were expressed by the group receiving information about the source after reading the message, whereas the attitudes of the group receiving immediate information about the source were less favorable. Delayed identification also resulted in increased shifts in attitude.

■ In those situations where the speaker has low credibility, all is not necessarily lost. Low credibility can be overcome if the speaker argues against his or her own best interests. In addition, the negative impact of low credibility can be reduced by identifying the speaker after he or she has presented the message. If the listener believes in advance that the speaker is unreliable or untrustworthy, the tendency is also to discount the information as being worthless. Delayed identification of a low-credibility source may thus enhance the persuasiveness of the message.

8.4 Being tall does not seem automatically to enhance a speaker's credibility.

One cultural truism held somewhat widely is that tall people appear more authoritative and are thus more credible than short people. However, what research has been done in this area seems to indicate that tallness does not necessarily give a public speaker a natural advantage in persuasive situations. Apparently, no direct relationship exists between tallness and effectiveness of a speaker.

Abstract

Eldon E. Baker and W. Charles Redding, "The Effects of Perceived Tallness in Persuasive Speaking," *Journal of Communication,* Vol. 12 (March 1962), pp. 51–53.

Baker and Redding attempted to discover whether a speaker perceived as tall would have a significant natural advantage in a persuasive speaking situation over one perceived as short. A professional photographer produced two pictures of the same speaker in such a manner that 87 beginning speech students judged the person in the "tall" photograph to be significantly taller than the person in the "short" photograph. The persuasive stimulus consisted of an 11-minute speech on the social acceptance and legality of euthanasia. A weighted graphic scale with seven intervals was used to measure pre- and postattitudes toward the position advocated in the speech.

In the study 123 experimental subjects and 44 controlled subjects were first administered the preattitude scale. Based on responses, experimental subjects were divided into two equally matched groups. Two days after the administration of the preattitude scale, both experimental groups heard the recorded speech. One group was exposed to the "tall speaker" and the other to the "short speaker." Perceptions of tall and short were influenced by experimenter's suggesting that the speaker was a tall fellow who played basketball and also by visual display of the photographs. An opaque projector was used to project the pictures so that all subjects could view them easily. After listening to the speech and being administered the postattitude scale, they were asked to indicate on a one-item questionnaire whether the talk had influenced them in any way, regardless of how they had marked the test. On the same day, the postattitude scale was also administered to the control group.

Both experimental groups shifted toward the speaker's position, but the only significant change was in the group who perceived the speaker as tall. However, the difference in the means on the postattitude scale between the two groups was not significant. Approximately the same percentage of subjects in both experimental groups testified that they were influenced toward the speaker's position. Baker and Redding concluded that tallness does not necessarily give a public speaker a significant natural advantage in a persuasive situation.

■ Tradition to the contrary, the research on tallness suggests that short men may not be at any natural disadvantage in a persuasive situation. Apparently one's height is not a direct influence on his credibility or persuasiveness.

8.5 Being male does seem to naturally enhance a speaker's credibility.

Some research has indicated that women are significantly more persuasible than men (Scheidel, 1963). However, some of the efforts to study the differences between men and women's susceptibility to influence suggests a different sort of relationship. Whittaker (1965) discovered that all subjects, regardless of sex, were persuaded to a greater degree when they were paired with a male as opposed to a female. He concluded that male sources are possibly more persuasive than female sources, regardless of the issue involved, the media used, or the sex of the receivers. Being male does appear to enhance a speaker's credibility.

Abstract

Gerald R. Miller and Michael McReynolds, "Male Chauvinism and Source Competence: A Research Note," *Speech Monographs*, Vol. 40 (June 1973), pp. 154–155.

Miller and McReynolds attempted to discover whether receivers of a message would rate a male communicator as more competent than a female communicator even if all other source qualifications and message content were held constant. In the study 69 male and 40 female undergraduates, who were enrolled in a great-issues course on war and peace, were administered an attitude pretest scale, which indicated almost all the subjects strongly opposed the development of an expanded ABM missile system. Each person read a message that was represented as a press release from a regional conference of nuclear scientists and contained arguments favoring an expanded ABM system. In both cases the source was identified as a Ph.D. in nuclear physics who was a director of a radiology laboratory and a scientific adviser to the National Security Council. The male source was identified as Dr. Robert Stapleton, with the masculine pronoun "he" occurring twice in the introduction, while the female source was identified as Dr. Gretchen Stapleton, with the feminine pronoun "she" occurring twice in the introduction. Identical in all other respects, these introductions and the persuasive message itself, were randomly distributed to the subjects. After reading the message, all subjects responded to two semantic differential-type scales used to measure perceived source competence. Pre- and posttests of attitudes toward the message topic were also administered.

The data revealed that competence ratings for the male source were higher, with female subjects rating Dr. Robert Stapleton slightly higher than the males did and significantly more competent than Dr. Gretchen Stapleton. Examination of the attitude-change scores revealed small, nonsignificant shifts. This, of course, was not surprising, given an issue where subjects expressed intensely negative attitudes at the start.

■ The evidence seems quite convincing that males have a natural advantage over females in terms of perceived credibility. Such differences may be a function of cultural training and expectations that may now be in the process of changing. As cultural expectations change, the findings of this research may also change. At the present time, little research has been done with female subjects on the effectiveness of female communicators on a female-oriented topic, like women's rights. Such a study might show significantly different results.

8.6   If an individual is perceived as attractive to the person being persuaded, he or she will tend to bring about a greater change in attitude.

Source attractiveness, like other complex concepts, has several dimensions, perhaps including some that have not been identified. *Familiarity, similarity,* and *liking* seem to be major factors in defining attractiveness (McGuire, 1969). These aspects of attraction are no doubt highly interrelated and may function sequentially, with similarity leading to familiarity and familiarity leading to liking, or vice versa. At a minimum, they mutually strengthen each other. Research on attractiveness has focused on one or more of these concepts. Mills and Aronson (1965) discovered that an attractive communicator's frankly stated desire to influence an audience was more productive than any other attribute and enhanced his or her effectiveness, while a similar desire expressed by an unattractive communicator resulted in a decrease in effectiveness. Wright (1966) experimented with a communication network in which one member of the chain could only pass messages to another. Through the use of notes, feelings of like or dislike were induced between participants and an experimental confederate, who sent written messages to attempt to persuade the subjects to lower their opinions of intercollegiate athletics—a topic on which they had expressed positive opinions. An attempt to influence by a liked person was more effective than from a disliked person. In this study efforts to persuade were also found useless unless the person liked the source of the message in the first place. Mills (1966) discovered that a speaker was rated as more friendly and less hostile when members of the audience felt he or she liked them. Subjects' impression of the communicator's friendliness and attractiveness was higher when persuasion took place. Agreement was also higher. Conversely, the desire to influence seemingly decreased the effectiveness of an unattractive communicator.

Abstract

Timothy C. Brock, "Communicator Recipient Similarity and Decision Change," *Journal of Personality and Social Psychology,* Vol. 1 (1965), pp. 650–654.

This study attempted to discover whether a persuader perceived in some way as similar to a recipient could produce more behavioral change than one perceived as an expert on a product. Two salesmen–communicators attempted to influence customers to buy either a higher or a lower priced paint. Their appeals were based on experience with using the paint and similarity to the customer regarding the amount of paint to be purchased. With half the sample, the salesmen were perceived as similar but inexperienced and with the other half they were perceived as dissimilar but experienced. In the study 22 subjects participated in each of the four conditions—higher price, lower price, similar, and dissimilar.

Both salesmen–communicators obtained the same pattern of outcomes. The results indicated that the dissimilar communicator, although presumably perceived as more knowledgable, was less effective than the communicator whose paint consumption was the same as the purchaser's.

■ Apparently, under the pressure of persuasion, people tend to change their opinions and behavior in the direction the communicator desires if they share some similarity in this area. The communicator who is familiar, similar, or liked—in other words, is attractive—will have a higher probability of influencing others to change. If we are attempting to persuade others, we must try to be perceived, then, as attractive to them.

Summary

A wide variety of individual factors influence our efforts to exert control over changes in the attitudes and behaviors of others. Persuasion and changing attitudes are complex processes with numerous obstacles. However, we can expect to be more successful in achieving this goal if we are viewed as having high credibility, which is increased by an organized, fluently presented message. Credibility, conversely, is reduced when we are perceived as being disorganized or when our presentation includes numerous nonfluencies. Low credibility can be counteracted by arguing against something that appears to be in our self-interest or by making sure that the source of the message is not identified until after the message has been received by the audience. Being tall does not seem automatically to enhance a speaker's credibility, but being male does. In addition, if we are perceived as being attractive to the person being persuaded, the likelihood is considerably greater that we will be able to be successful in our persuasive efforts.

Background Readings

The process of achieving change in people relies upon the influence of individuals, groups, and social processes. Discussions of persuasion usually attempt to integrate or at least examine each set of variables in a single treatise. Thus, the suggested background readings in this part and chapter consist of segments drawn from larger volumes.

Cronkhite, Gary, *Persuasion: Speech and Behavioral Change* (Indianapolis: The Bobbs-Merrill Co., 1969), Chapter 8, "The Persuader's Choices." This chapter analyzes the decisions that a persuader must make, the alternatives available, and the circumstances under which each alternative should be chosen. The choices having to do with selected sources and motivations are most directly related to individual factors in change.

Ehninger, Douglas, *Influence, Belief, and Argument* (Glenview, Ill.: Scott, Foresman and Co., 1974). The subtitle of this book is *An Introduction to Responsible Persuasion.* The general orientation of approach and materials is toward changing the personal beliefs of individuals. It deals with proof, evidence, argument, and the propositions they support.

Hovland, Carl I., and Irving L. Janis, eds., *Personality and Persuasibility* (New Haven, Conn.: Yale University Press, 1959). This book reports research on the relationships between personality variables and persuasibility. The emphasis is on the correlation of consistent individual differences with responsiveness to persuasive messages.

Karlins, Marvin, and Herbert I. Abelson, *Persuasion: How Opinions and Attitudes Are Changed,* 2nd ed. (New York: Springer Publishing Co., 1970.) Two chapters of this summary of research on propositions concerning persuasion are related to individual factors: "The Audience as Individuals" and "The Persuader."

Miller, Gerald R., and Michael Burgoon, *New Techniques of Persuasion* (New York: Harper & Row, 1973). A chapter on inducing resistance to persuasion discusses individual persuadee differences and ways of increasing resistance to persuasive attempts.

9.1   People with a strong sense of belonging to a group tend to be influenced more by that group than those not having such feelings.

9.2   If the group establishes standards for acceptable ways of behaving, the behavior of its members will be subsequently influenced.

9.3   By rewarding those who conform to the standards of the group and punishing those who deviate from them, small groups can produce change in their members.

9.4   By stating opinions acceptable to a group or by participating in group discussion, individuals make a public commitment that influences them to hold the group's position even in private.

9.5   If individuals participate in group decision making, they will be willing to take a greater risk in making individual decisions.

9.6   Individuals who participate in group brainstorming processes tend to produce more and higher quality solutions.

Chapter 9
Small Group Factors

The study of small groups has led us to believe that the behavior, attitudes, feelings, and beliefs of individuals are most often anchored in the groups to which they belong. With rare, if any, exceptions everyone belongs to at least several groups, which influence how each person acts, feels, and believes; in turn, these individuals influence how the group functions and changes. Cartwright (1954) has pointed out that, in the first instance, the group is viewed as a source of influence over its members. Any attempt to change individual behavior, for example, can be facilitated or hindered by means of pressure stemming from the group. In the second instance, the individual exerts pressure on other group members so as to change the group itself. Thus, individuals act on and produce changes in group standards, the overall or feeling climate of the group, the leadership-member relationship, or the organizational structure of the group. Also, a third kind of influence may be possible, even necessary at times. The group may be changed directly, not incidentally as individuals interact with one another and these individual changes influence the group. Efforts to change are directed toward the group as a unit rather than at individual members, as in the second instance. The group itself becomes a target of change.

In this chapter, we shall be concerned primarily with how groups influence the behavior of individuals. The research related to the influence of groups on individual behavior has been summarized under the topical category of *conformity*.

Kiesler and Kiesler (1969) define *conformity* as ". . . a change in behavior or belief toward a group as a result of real or imagined group pressure." This change toward a group means that as individuals influence one another, they become increasingly like each other in attitude and action, with the group as a result becoming somewhat uniform in belief and behavior.

There are, of course, conditions under which group pressure and influence seem to fail. Such conditions produce people who seem to respond independently as *nonconformists*. However, careful analysis may discover that these nonconformists are simply conforming to an unknown group. Assuming that there may be some true nonconformists, Jahoda (1959) makes the point that nonconformity and independence are probably as important to understand as conformity. As Jahoda demonstrates, however, an examination of the evidence on factors influencing conforming behavior also reveals much about nonconforming inclinations.

Predictive Propositions

9.1 People with a strong sense of belonging to a group tend to be influenced more by that group than those not having such feelings.

The influence of a group will be greater when a member feels strongly that he or she is an accepted part of the group (Back, 1956). To be able to exert an influence over its members, a group must have power, which represents the ability to bring forces to bear on a person so he or she will think and act like the others. The existence of power results in *cohesiveness*. To attain strong cohesiveness, members of a group must express positive and cooperative attitudes toward one another and toward the task to be accomplished. A strong sense of belonging means that they are experiencing a high level of cohesiveness. The power of a group may be measured in respect to how attractive it is to its members. If a person wants to be a permanent member, he or she will be more easily influenced by that group. A member will also be more willing to conform to group rules and guidelines. Marlow and Jergen (1969) assert that "the principle that members who are highly attracted to a group are also most likely to conform is well established for many social settings."

A strong sense of belonging to a group is influenced by the extent to which a member is attracted to that group or values his membership, along with the extent by which he feels that others in the group value his membership. Festinger, Schachter, and Back (1950) demonstrated that the more highly a person is attracted to a group, the more he tends to conform to the face-to-face pressures operating within the group. Dittes and Kelley (1956) studied the effects of different degrees of acceptance by group members on a person's conformity to the group's norms. The degree of acceptance was measured by having subjects rate one another anonymously on how desirable it was to keep each person in a discussion group. Results revealed that the ratings produced noticeable differences in perceived acceptance. The very low-rated subjects viewed being rejected from the group as very likely. Subjects who valued the group and who, though less than completely accepted by the group, had some possibility of achieving complete acceptance, found that conformity in both private and public statements and behavior served to facilitate such approval. Conversely, subjects on the verge of unwanted rejection demonstrated conformity only at the public level, supposedly as a means of delaying their rejection from the group.

Abstract

Stanley Schachter, Norris Ellertson, Dorothy McBride, and Doris Gregory, "An Experimental Study of Cohesiveness and Productivity," *Human Relations*, Vol. 4 (1951), pp. 229–238.

This study explored whether attempts to influence group members to higher or lower production would be more effective in groups high in cohesion or low in cohesion. Subjects were divided into groups of three unacquainted female subjects, who were given the task of producing cardboard checkerboards. Instructions to each group were that one member was to cut the cardboard, another mount and paste it on heavier stock, and the third paint the board through a stencil. Speed and quantity of production were stressed. Secretly, however, each subject was assigned to the job of cutting. Communication between subjects could be only by notes delivered by a messenger. Although they could write as many notes as they pleased, they were unaware that all notes were intercepted and standard prewritten ones substituted. Every four minutes the messenger delivered and collected notes and the cardboard that each subject had finished. After subjects cut cardboard for 32 minutes, they completed a questionnaire and were debriefed.

Messages (notes) asking for increased production did increase productivity, but no significant difference existed between high and low cohesive groups. When the notes urged a slowdown in production, the subjects in high cohesive groups constantly decreased production. The results generally supported the hypothesis that cohesion, attractiveness of a group to its members, is directly related to the degree of influence each member has on the other. Generally, high cohesion groups were more successful than those of low cohesion in increasing or decreasing productivity.

■ There appears to be little question that groups do exert influence on their members that can and does result in somewhat uniform patterns of behavior. Pressures toward conformity seem quite strong in those groups where the members have a sense of belonging and a high level of cohesiveness. Both the pressures toward conformity and cohesiveness are exerted by means of some communication process. Thus, cohesion, conformity, and communication are interrelated, affecting the ways in which small groups produce changes in people. If members develop a strong sense of belonging to the group, the group can more easily influence their attitudes and behavior.

9.2 If the group establishes standards for acceptable ways of behaving, the behavior of its members will be subsequently influenced.

Most of us learn a great deal about how to behave properly through the small groups to which we belong. The rules that specify and make certain kinds of behavior legitimate are called *norms* and, for the most part, are derived from the goals of the group. Hare (1962) explains that "given a set of goals, norms define the kind of behavior which is necessary for or consistent with the realization of those goals."

Asch (1965), experimenting on the effects of group pressure on individual judgments, was able to produce a temporary group norm by having all members of a group, except one—the subject—serve as confederates who would give unanimous but incorrect judgments on the length of lines at which all group members looked. Asch had the majority place the subject in a position in which, although he was giving correct responses, he was faced with a unanimous opinion, or norm, directly opposed to his judgment. In each case, the subject could go along with the rest of the group (since he was giving his answers last), or he could repudiate the group members. Interestingly, a considerable percentage of the subjects yielded to the group pressure and denied the evidence of their own senses.

Apparently, a cohesive group that has developed a standard of behavior may exert strong pressures on members to conform to the group norm. In this study group pressure through norms aided the group in accomplishing its goals and helped members maintain unity. Such norms can also help the members of a group make decisions about problems that have no basis in objective reality, such as what is more beautiful or useful; norms further help members to define and understand a group's relationship to other groups, organizations, and institutions in society. All of these reasons serve valuable ends, making consensus and conformity an indispensable condition of life with others. However, independence of thought and action are also essential commodities for improving group decisions.

Thorndyke (1938) discovered that students who first make value judgments of pictures, poems, and other artistic creations and then discuss their decisions in small groups, tend to alter their early judgments to conform with the majority opinion of those groups. He concluded that group discussion and majority opinion were highly related to shifts in individual members' judgments. Such conformity occurs not only in laboratory experiments, but also in real-life situations. Lefkowitz, Blake, and Mouton (1955) had a confederate–model obey and violate traffic signals on different street corners. The confederate both obeyed and violated the signals. In 526 instances the confederate led violations 52 times, while, when he obeyed signals, they were violated only 4 times in 771 instances.

Abstract

John Downing, "Cohesiveness, Perception, and Values," *Human Relations,* Vol. 11 (1958), pp. 157–166.

Downing was concerned with how cohesiveness and group opinions would affect individual judgments and whether such judgments would tend to converge toward that of a group standard or norm. In this study, each subject was asked to estimate how far a dot of light moved in a dark room, first working individually and then working in groups in which the other members were experimenter-confederates. Group cohesion was manipulated by telling subjects either that they would like other members and be liked in return or that they would not. Two types of group pressure were employed: *positive,* which attempted to increase a subject's estimates on the dot's movements by announcing group estimates as being about 50% higher than those of individual subjects who initially worked alone; and *negative*, which attempted to decrease a subject's estimates by putting group estimates at about 50% lower than the initial estimates of individual subjects. After the group sessions, subjects were administered a questionnaire asking whether they would like to become better acquainted with the other members of the study.

The degree of induced cohesion did not seem to be directly related to the conformity of subjects to the group judgment, although individuals in high cohesion groups wanted to know their group members better than did subjects in low cohesion groups. Regardless, in all instances, the pressure exerted by confederates resulted in increased conformity by the subjects, regardless of whether the pressure was to increase or decrease initial judgments.

■ Members of a small group are able to influence the behavior of other members directly. This influence often occurs by setting norms for acceptable ways of behaving, with the group exerting pressure to conform to these real or contrived standards. The communication of such norms results in a direct influence on the behavior and attitudes of individual members. In other words, groups can be used to change individuals.

9.3   By rewarding those who conform to the standards of the group and punishing those who deviate from them, small groups can produce change in their members.

When the individual's behavior is consistent with group norms and expectations, that behavior will be received with approval. On the other hand, when the member discovers that his or her behavior is different from that expected by the group, he or she has these options: change behavior and conform to the norms, change the norms, continue as a deviant from the norms, leave the group, or be ejected from the group. The research indicates that the deviant members of a group are more likely to change their behavior to meet the standards of the group than the group is likely to change toward the deviant members. They find that conformity is enforced by such common techniques as ridicule, ostracism, and, on occasion, even violence. The violation of even minor customs often arouses a reaction. Miller and Form (1951) recounted the story of a strawboss of a labor gang who wore an old cloth cap on the job. One day he appeared wearing a light grey Stetson. The workers razzed him and asked if he thought he was a big boss. He offered some excuse but reappeared the next day with the Stetson. Again, the workers reacted, but more violently than on the previous day. On the third day, the strawboss arrived on the job with his old hat. Roethlisberger and Dickson (1939) discovered a strong tendency to keep production within the capacity of the average worker. Where there are highly cohesive groups, the group will enforce both minimum and maximum standards of work.

The academic community is not immune to intolerance and deviant positions either. Rice (1973) reviewed the case of Arthur Jensen, respected educational psychologist at the University of California at Berkeley, who published an article suggesting that heredity may have more effect than environment on determining intelligence. One implication of Jensen's research was that compensatory educational programs, such as Head Start, that focus on enriching the environment could not offset the effect of heredity. Although the article was published in a professional journal, public mass media came out with stories playing up the racial overtones rather than the scientific hypothesis and data. Press interpretations included distortions, misstatements, omissions, and assimilations much akin to the changes that occur in the serial transmission of information (see Chapter 7). Readers, of course, added their own interpretations. The result was a torrent of letters to editors denouncing Jensen and urging punishments ranging from censure to hanging.

On the California campus, rallies were held with sound trucks calling for the university to fire Jensen; handbills warned that Jensen must perish. A formal resolution was introduced into the academic senate calling for an investigation. Campus demonstrators invaded his classes and prevented him from speaking at other universities. At a national convention, other demonstrators invaded the speaker's platform, tore up the speech Jensen was preparing to deliver, and threw it in his face. Such is the rage of the community when a single person or a minority speaks in opposition to majority customs or holds unpopular ideologies.

Pressures toward conformity have been studied in the laboratory as well as observed in real life. Festinger and Thibaut (1951) discovered that messages in small groups tended to be directed toward members whose opinions were quite deviant. Under conditions of high pressure toward uniformity and perceived homogeneity, the tendency to direct messages to members holding extreme opinions increased.

Our discussion thus far has focused on the use of punitive control over deviant members of groups. However, the group, while supporting the opinions and behaviors of its conforming members, may simply ignore the nonconformists. Calvin (1962) had 24 members of an introductory psychology class, from a campus with about 500 coeds, provide simple verbal reinforcement (compliments) to all women wearing blue clothes on specified days. Reinforcement was later changed to coeds wearing red clothes. The findings revealed that prior to reinforcement, about 25% of the coeds dressed in blue outfits. After reinforcement, the figure rose to 35%. Coeds wearing red clothes moved from 11% prior to reinforcement to 22% afterwards. These kinds of results demonstrate the influence of groups in producing changes in attitudes and behaviors through both rewards and punishments.

Abstract

Stanley Schachter, "Deviation, Rejection, and Communication," *Journal of Abnormal and Social Psychology*, Vol. 46 (1951), pp. 190–207.

Schachter was interested in discovering the different kinds of communicative behavior that would occur in small groups toward varying degrees of deviants. For the experiment four different types of small clubs were organized by recruiting male college students to participate. Eight groups of five to seven members of each club type were studied (32 groups total). In each group—deviating from or conforming to an experimentally created group standard—were three paid confederates called the *deviant,* the *slider,* and the *mode.* After being asked to read a case history of a juvenile delinquent awaiting sentencing for a minor crime, members of the groups participated in a 45-minute discussion about what each thought should be done. At the end of 20 minutes, each leader took a census to insure that everybody was aware of everyone else's position.

During the discussion period in each club, an observer introduced as a friend of the leader and interested in what the club was doing recorded the following: who spoke to whom; the time each interaction took; whether the speaker attacked or supported the position of the person to whom he spoke; whether a comment, even if not addressed to a person with a specific viewpoint, implied approval or disapproval of the position; and whether the speaker talked about experiences from his own personal history or from a friend's.

All groups took a modal position toward love and understanding; the deviate and slider in each group, however, favored extreme discipline. Though the deviate maintained the same position throughout, the slider eventually allowed himself to be influenced and changed his position to concur with the majority. The third confederate, the mode, agreed with the majority position from the start.

At the conclusion of the discussion, a final census was taken and each subject filled out committee-nomination blanks and sociometric questionnaires before being debriefed. Sociometric data indicated that group members in mode and slider roles were not rejected, but the deviate was

definitely rejected—the degree of rejection being greater in highly cohesive groups. Initially, statements were directed primarily toward the deviate and the slider, but decreased toward the slider as he approached the majority opinion. Communication toward the deviate increased up to a point and then decreased, but was most pronounced by those who rejected him. The general pattern seemed to be one of vigorous attempts to get the deviate and the slider to conform, followed by complete acceptance of the one who conformed and complete rejection of the one who refused. Shaw (1971) observes that "the moral of this story seems to be that it's all right to be a deviate, so long as you are 'flexible enough' to change your mind when the majority of the group points out the 'error of your ways.'"

■ Groups often do exert pressure upon their members to conform to their established standards and norms. These pressures take the form of reward, such as compliments and praise for conforming behavior and punishment, such as criticism or censure, for nonconforming behavior. Such group efforts are usually successful in influencing deviates to change their behavior.

9.4 By stating opinions acceptable to a group or by participating in group discussion, individuals make a public commitment that influences them to hold the group's position even in private.

As a general rule, opinions that people make known to others are more difficult to repudiate than those they hold privately. It follows that a person is more likely to change public opinion and/or behavior if he or she goes on record as a deviant in a group, especially a group to which he or she is highly attracted. Opinions stated in public are often different from those we hold privately. However, if we express an opinion or mention an intended behavior publicly, our *actual* behavior is more likely to be consistent with our public statement than if we only hold the opinion privately. Pressure exerted on us to express publicly an opinion different from the one we hold privately tends to influence us to state the acceptable opinion while rejecting the idea privately. However, if we desire to continue in a group favoring the publicly held opinion, we are likely to change our private opinion so that it is consistent with both the public and group viewpoint. This may occur because of a desire for consistency or because we do not wish to be rejected from the group (Bandura, 1969, p. 613). Under such circumstances consistency is often maintained through external, social influence rather than internal mental compromises.

Research has amply demonstrated the powerful effect of public statement and commitment on later public and private opinions and behavior. Gordon (1952) asked 24 males living in a boarding house to record privately their individual opinions on a particular topic. Each subject was then asked to express an opinion on the same topic publicly where the other members of the group could easily hear him. Immediately afterwards, each person was asked to rate his opinion of the group. Subjects tended to conform to their conception of the group's opinion when giving their public opinion, which typically was a compromise between each person's private opinion and his conception of the group's opinion. Mouton, Blake, and Olmstead (1956) used the basic research design of Asch, but varied the stimulus from visual lines to clicks of a metronome. Half of the subjects were asked to give their names before giving each of their judgments; the other half remained anonymous. When subjects identified themselves, 14 yielded to the group judgment 3 or more times, while only 4 yielded when they remained anonymous. Apparently, individuals are more committed to their public statements and behavior than those that are private. In addition, they often modify their public statements to fit their perception of the group's opinion.

Abstract

Bertram H. Raven, "Social Influence on Opinions and the Communication of Related Content," *Journal of Abnormal and Social Psychology,* Vol. 58 (1959), pp. 119–128.

Raven was interested in the effect of group pressure on opinion when a member held an opinion privately but the possibilities for being rejected for nonconformity were greater. A total of 344 subjects were divided into homogeneous groups of from 10 to 14 individuals. To increase cohesiveness, only those expressing an interest in the subject matter were used, and they participated in a short group discussion to stimulate interest prior to the experiment. Each subject was given a case study of a juvenile arrested for the robbery and murder of an elderly lady. Interviews with his mother, the boy himself, and his teacher were presented with each providing contradictory information about the offender and his crime. When the initial reading was completed, subjects were told their opinions would be kept private and not be communicated to fellow group members; then they were asked to indicate these opinions on a 7-point scale measuring the extent to which they felt the boy was personally responsible for the crime.

To make the subjects feel that they were deviates from a well-defined group norm, the experimenter reported, by marking X's opposite scale positions, a false consensus at the personal responsibility end of the scale. There was a general reaction of shocked surprise to this consensus, since most subjects chose opinions at the environmental responsibility end of the scale. They were then told to write a group report on the case with which everyone must agree completely. After rereading the case, they were asked for a second statement of opinion, which once again was privately solicited. As an aid in writing the group report, subjects were also asked to write individual descriptions of the case as they saw it before being requested to state their private opinions a third time. A questionnaire was then administered to test the effectiveness of the public–private manipulation. A false consensus seemed effective in impressing subjects with the belief that they were deviates.

A significantly larger proportion of the deviates shifted their final statements of opinion toward the group norm, even though they could keep these private. Deviates whose descriptions were read by others more often changed their opinions than those whose descriptions could be kept private. Subjects holding less extreme positions prepared public descriptions more supportive of the group norm than their private ones. The greatest distortion occurred when rejection was a possibility and a person's statement was to be made public.

■ When individuals can be influenced to make public statements or public commitments, the likelihood is great that these will be closer to the group's position than any privately held opinion. In addition, a public commitment will most often result in a change in the private attitude or opinion—most often toward the group's position. Individuals tend to conform by selecting and distorting the content communicated so as to avoid rejection from the group. The more an individual must communicate regarding his or her opinion, the greater the pressure appears to be to change that opinion toward the group's position.

9.5 If individuals participate in group decision making, they will be willing to take a greater risk in making individual decisions.

The group atmosphere may free members of a group to consider decisions that are more risky, uninhibited, and bolder than those they might consider when working independently as individuals. The group atmosphere has the potential of creating a situation in which judgment can be suspended, and creative, bold, and even radical ideas may be considered in making decisions. The concept of risky decisions has been studied on several occasions with the tentative conclusion that decisions made by groups may be riskier than prediscussion decisions that individual members of the group make. If a relationship exists between quality of decisions and their boldness and riskiness, then the influence of the group toward greater individual risk taking could enhance both individual and group decisions. Research has generally demonstrated that the tendency toward riskier decisions by groups is a real phenomenon.

Abstract

Michael A. Wallach, Nathan Kogan, and Daryl J. Bem, "Group Influence on Individual Risk Taking," *Journal of Abnormal and Social Psychology,* Vol. 65 (1962), pp. 75–86.

This study was an attempt to determine to what degree group decisions might be riskier than individual decisions. It also focused on whether the group's effect on risk would be limited only to its members' overt compliance or would also extend to their private acceptance and decision making.

Finally, the study explored the extent to which the group's effect on risk would be enduring.

A total of 167 subjects—14 all-male groups and 14 all-female groups —participated in the study in groups of 6 people each, none of whom was previously acquainted. Seated around a table in a seminar room, subjects in individual groups were told they were to complete the Wallach-Kogan-Bem Choice

Dilemma Questionnaire, consisting of descriptions of 12 hypothetical situations. In each situation the central figure or character must choose between two courses of action, one of which is more risky than the other, but also more rewarding if successful. The subject's task, the experimenter explained, was to indicate the lowest probability of success that he or she would accept before recommending the potentially more rewarding alternative. The experimenter also emphasized that the more risky alternative is always assumed to be more desirable. This example is a typical situation: "A college senior with considerable musical talent must choose between the secure course of going on to medical school and becoming a physician or the risky course of embarking on a career as a concert pianist." After the subjects responded to the questionnaire individually, they discussed each situation as a group and by consensus arrived at a decision. Then members, individually and privately, indicated their own personal decisions again in order to measure what influence the group decision might have had on these. After discussing their individual decisions, each participant ranked all the subjects in his group, including himself, as to how much each person influenced the final group decision, then ranked everyone except himself as to how much he would like to become better acquainted with everyone in his group. Some subjects were asked to return two to six weeks later, reconsider the situations,

and complete the choice-dilemma questionnaire a third time.

Compared with the risk levels the subjects indicated in their first individual decisions, the results following group discussions, in which members tried to arrive at a consensus, indicated a strong move toward greater risk taking. This move was essentially the same for females as for males. The second individual decisions following discussion also showed a strong move toward greater risk taking. This group discussion process seemed to have as significant an effect on privately held attitudes as it did on publicly expressed views. The degree of risk an individual was willing to recommend seemed unrelated to the popularity a person had within a group. Shifts in the risky direction seemed to be maintained over the subsequent period of time. In the control group where no group discussion occurred, no shift toward greater risk taking seemed to occur.

■ In regard to risk taking, then, involvement in group discussion and achievement of consensus can result in a willingness to make more risky decisions than those made without such interaction. Moreover, after group discussions, the willingness to take risks seems to continue even when an individual is once again making private decisions. Small groups can enhance decision making and contribute to bolder, more exciting and creative problem solving.

9.6   Individuals who participate in group brainstorming processes tend to produce more and higher quality solutions.

The personal feeling that five heads are more likely to produce a better solution to a problem than one alone has gained support through empirical research. Investigators of individual-versus-group problem solving abilities have used a wide variety of experimental designs, but the results show remarkably consistent support for the superiority of group over individual problem solving. One technique for assisting a group to produce more and higher quality solutions to problems is that of *brainstorming*. In brainstorming procedures participants are asked to express any possible solutions that come to mind during the initial phase of finding ideas to solve problems; evaluation of these ideas is postponed to a later time. A large number of ideas are sought by encouraging participants to combine and elaborate upon others' ideas and to offer these ideas without qualitative judgments. The evidence suggests strongly that brainstorming procedures lead to more solutions of higher quality than do problem-solving procedures not using the brainstorming philosophy. In addition, participating in brainstorming procedures seems to influence individual members to create and present more and higher quality solutions than they normally would while functioning independently of the group.

Abstract

Arnold Meadow, Sidney J. Parnes, and Hayne Reese, "Influence of Brainstorming Instructions and Problem Sequence on a Creative Problem-Solving Test," *Journal of Applied Psychology,* Vol. 43 (1959), pp. 413–416.

Basically, this study attempted to determine whether more and better ideas would develop from brainstorming procedures than from more traditional problem-solving procedures requiring subjects to formulate and evaluate solutions simultaneously. In the experiment 32 students from two courses in creative problem solving were randomly divided into four experimental groups of eight individuals each and given two problems to solve. The problems required that subjects list other than conventional uses for a hanger and a broom. All participants completed both tasks individually; half of them were given the hanger problem first, then the broom problem. For the others the problems were given in reverse. Likewise, half the subjects received the brainstorming instructions second while the other half got their instructions in reverse. Each idea suggestion was copied on a separate slip of paper, coded, and presented to a "blind" rater for an evaluation. The rater was never aware of whether he was scoring for a brainstorming or a nonbrainstorming idea. Each idea was rated on a three-point scale for uniqueness and value.

The data showed that more good solutions resulted from the brainstorming than the nonbrainstorming instructions and that the effect was greater in the first test period than the second. Individuals also created considerably more and better ideas in the brainstorming situation than they created individually.

■ Brainstorming techniques can help improve both the quantity and the quality of group decisions. The freedom created in the brainstorming situation appears to help individuals to create ideas that normally they do not think of when they are working alone. If we want to improve the quality and the quantity of decisions we must make, then participating in brainstorming can be an effective device.

Summary

The behavior, attitudes, feelings, and beliefs of individuals are anchored in the groups to which they belong. Changes in individuals often occur because of group influence. People who have a strong sense of belonging to a group tend to be influenced more by the group than those without this feeling. Group cohesiveness and attractiveness result in individuals' attempting to conform to group standards.

As a matter of fact, groups influence the behavior of members by setting standards for acceptable ways of behaving. They also produce change in members by rewarding those conforming to group standards and punishing those deviating from them. Privately held opinions and attitudes can be shifted toward the group's position if an individual can be influenced to commit himself publicly on those opinions and attitudes. Groups also influence the quality and nature of decisions made by their members. Participation in group decision making can make an individual more willing to make risky decisions, as well as increase both the quantity and the quality of solutions he or she might produce alone.

Background Readings

The literature on small groups is so vast that one could easily pick out a respectable treatment of group theory and practice in almost any office on campus. The issues relating to change and groups center on how a group improves individual performance and increases conformity to group goals. These recent books on small group behavior provide both general and specific analyses of those issues.

Applbaum, Ronald L., Edward M. Bodaken, Kenneth K. Sereno, and Karl W. E. Anatol, *The Process of Group Communication* (Palo Alto, Calif.: Science Research Associates, 1974). This book examines problem solving, norms, cohesiveness, conflict, and leadership as they are affected by groups.

Davis, James H., *Group Performance* (Reading, Mass.: Addison-Wesley Publishing Co., 1969). This short book summarizes research on such aspects of group performance as decision making, problem solving, productivity, and goal attainment.

Jacobson, Wally D., *Power and Interpersonal Relations* (Belmont, Calif.: Wadsworth Publishing Co., 1972). This overview of the role of power in human interaction is based on small group research. It treats power from points of view of agents and recipients—and of methods used in actualizing power.

Kiesler, Charles A., and Sara B. Kiesler, *Conformity* (Reading, Mass.: Addison-Wesley Publishing Co., 1969). This is a companion volume to Davis (see above) and treats topics such as group pressure, compliance, and private endorsement.

Patton, Bobby R., and Kim Giffin, *Problem-Solving Group Interaction* (New York: Harper & Row, 1973). This book contains both an introduction to group theory and a detailed analysis of the problem-solving process.

Rosenfeld, Lawrence B., *Human Interaction in the Small Group Setting* (Columbus, Ohio: Charles E. Merrill Publishing Co., 1973). This is an overall review of small group theory, with specific chapters on group influence, leadership, attraction, and conflict resolution.

10.1 The process by which people accept new ideas involves a complex series of acts that can be divided into five steps for analysis: awareness, interest, evaluation, trial, and adoption.

10.2 The mass media arouse interest in new ideas, methods, and projects early in the adoption process; however, interpersonal communication is especially influential in the actual decision to adopt.

10.3 Individuals tend to adopt new ideas at different times, but they fall into one of five time-of-adoption categories: innovators, early adopters, early majority, late majority, and laggards.

10.4 The use of television advertising is a form of social action that can produce decisions leading to the sale of a product.

10.5 Instigating change in social systems requires implementing a series of clearly defined steps that mark the progress of an idea from conception to implementation.

Chapter 10
Social Action Factors

Social action is the process by which decisions are made about new ideas in a community, an organization, or other social systems. Social action implies that the decision is arrived at collectively and applies to the activities of people who are members of a particular social system (Bettinghaus, 1973, pp. 248–249). We generally think of social action campaigns as involving the development of community support for a school bond for building a community recreation center, for changing from a city commission to a mayoral form of government, or for getting better lighting on a campus. Social action, as we are using the term, also includes changes such as adopting a competency-based educational system in a school district, getting a bike-way constructed in a community, encouraging farmers to adopt a new type of seed, running a political campaign, developing an advertising campaign to get people to recycle cans, carrying out a missionary program to elicit new converts to a religious group, or running a fund-raising drive for the United Crusade. Any activities in which individuals or groups of individuals ultimately accept a different way of doing something is a kind of social action.

Social action, as experience and research demonstrate, is the result of countless individual events involving both interpersonal and mass communication. It involves not only diffusing information but also influencing others through that information. One of the major concepts in social action is *adoption*—the actual putting a proposed action into practice. In 1974, our country experienced an energy shortage.

Special social action campaigns were created to get people to reduce their consumption of gasoline, oil, electricity, and other forms of energy. The purchase of small cars and bicycles, adoption of car pools, reduction in the number of miles traveled, lowering of thermostat settings, and use of fewer energy-consuming appliances were part of the overall program. Social action campaigns were created to bring about the adoption of these new practices, but such changes do not occur immediately; they take months or even years. Of course, social change is part of the human condition. Social action programs simply attempt to influence the rate at which that change occurs. Sometimes the process is slowed, sometimes it is accelerated, but there is always an attempt to change the process.

Since social action involves large groups of individuals, whole communities, or even nations, studies related to it do not lend themselves to the normal laboratory experiment. Instead, most of the research done has been through field studies and surveys. Therefore, in this chapter many of the propositions will not be of the *if–then* nature used earlier in this book. However, the propositions do attempt to describe some of the notions about social action that appear to be supported by the research already accomplished. We will discover that much of the research is descriptive, rather than prescriptive in nature, explaining what has occurred or is likely to occur rather than providing a scientific basis for prediction. However, such descriptive research often is essential in setting the stage for developing scientific predictions.

Predictive Propositions

10.1   The process by which people accept new ideas involves a complex series of acts that can be divided into five steps for analysis: awareness, interest, evaluation, trial, and adoption.

Generally, change in a community or an organization occurs somewhat spontaneously in response to members' felt needs for something new. Quite often, however, groups of individuals have become dissatisfied with the rather slow rate at which changes occur spontaneously and have attempted to develop strategies for planning change. University students, ethnic minorities, women, milk producers, and advertisers have sought to accelerate the rate at which changes might occur in organizations, communities, or nations. In adopting new ideas, people appear to have progressed through four prior stages; they first become *aware* of the idea or product, develop enough favorable *interest* in it to seek more information, then weigh the advantages and disadvantages in an effort to *evaluate* the efficacy of adopting it, *try* the product through small-scale use or adoption to determine its usefulness and finally fully adopt the new idea but still seek further information to confirm the wisdom of their choice. (These stages are based on an analysis by Everett M. Rogers, 1962.)

From the moment an individual becomes aware of an innovation until he decides to continue using it may involve a considerable period of time. Rogers notes that there were 40 years between the first successful use of the tunnel oven and its general use in the pottery industry; that it took more than 14 years for hybrid seed corn to find widespread use in Iowa; that more than 30 years passed between the first and last adopters of fertilizer in a Columbian village; and that it has taken 50 years for kindergarten to be adopted as part of the American public school system (and several states have not yet made such an adoption). Toffler (1970) writes that "we have in our time released a totally new social force—a stream of change so accelerated that it influences our sense of time, revolutionizes the tempo of daily life, and affects the very way we feel in 'the world around us.'" The term *future shock* was coined to describe the consequence of increased rates of change and that companion experience of transience, of time moving so fast that the rapid rate at which one innovation replaces another makes us unable to cope with our feeling of impermanence. This sense of future shock is an impelling reason to know more about social change and the action that brings it about.

Evidence on the five stage process of innovation adoption and social action that we discussed above is presented by Katz (1961) in an analysis of two studies of innovation diffusion—one concerning hybrid seed corn and the other, a new drug. His findings indicated that the pattern of adoption follows an S-shaped curve and implies there are characteristic stages in the adoption process. In both studies a spread in time from 3 to 13 years occurred between learning of the new product and its actual adoption by a large majority. Also, the results reveal that information alone was insufficient to influence a doctor or a farmer to adopt the innovation, leading to the conclusion that the adoption process is complex but perhaps can be analyzed by means of the five stages mentioned.

Abstract

George M. Beal, Everett M. Rogers, and Joe M. Bohlen, "Validity of the Concept of Stages in the Adoption Process," *Rural Sociology,* Vol. 22 (1957), pp. 166–168.

This study was designed to determine whether the five conceptualized stages in the adoption process could be validated empirically. In attempting such a test, the authors did not necessarily assume that there are only five possible stages, that these are discrete and mutually exclusive, or that the present conceptualization of the five is the best possible. Rather, the stages were taken as given, and the effort was to determine whether they existed as realities in the minds of people going through the adoption process.

The practice selected for testing the stages concept was the feeding of antibiotics to swine, a fairly new development at the time of the study. Subjects were 148 farmers who resided in the trade-area community of a central Iowa town and were also involved in a larger study of communication and the diffusion of farm practices. Questions were asked about information sources in each of the five assumed stages, as follows: (1) *Awareness:* Where or from whom did you first see or hear about the use of antibiotics in hog feed? (2) *Information:* After you first heard about antibiotics, where or from whom did you get additional, more detailed information about them? (3) *Application:* After you had adequate information about antibiotics, where or from whom did you get the information that helped you decide whether actually to try them on your own farm? (4) *Trial:* After you decided to try out antibiotics on your own farm, where or from whom did you get the most information or help on where to get them, the kind to use, how much to use, and how to feed them? (5) *Adoption:* After you once tried antibiotics on your own farm, how did you decide whether to continue using them—actually adopt them?

The authors felt that, if the stages were to have theoretical value, the vast majority of people—in this case, farmers—would go through each of the five when adopting a given practice. In general, the data from the study tended to validate the stages. One of the authors directed the field work and personally interviewed more than a fifth of the farmers. In his judgment most adopters of giving antibiotics were aware of going through a series of stages as they moved toward using the medication. They seemed to have little trouble recalling when they became aware of, tried, and adopted the practice. There were very few "don't know" or "don't remember" answers. Specifically, of the 105 farmers adopting the antibiotics, all, by their responses, indicated passing through the awareness, information, and application stages. Ten reported they had not gone through the trial stage on their own farms but had moved directly from application to adoption. However, several of these ten indicated that this stage is one they often go through, even though not in the case of antibiotics. If the farmers generally named message sources or combinations of sources for the different stages, this would seem to indicate some differentiation of the stages. When the message sources named for each stage were compared with those named for the next stage, it was found that in most cases different sources were given. A question could be raised about the validity of the stages concept if the farmers had stated that they adopted on impulse—that they became aware of antibiotics and adopted immediately. No farmer, however, reported that he adopted in this fashion. Instead, there was an average reported time lag of 1.54 years between awareness and adoption.

■ Though the findings reported here are not conclusive, they seem to support the validity of a stages concept. Analysis of similar data for three other practices studied in Iowa provided further supporting evidence. Seemingly, the adoption of a complex new practice by any individual is not a single isolated act. The adoption process is probably a specific application of the general pattern by which human beings learn to make changes of any kind. The stages discussed here apparently exist for most individuals as they go about adopting new procedures, ideas, or practices.

Social action appears to be a complex process involving a number of different steps. However, the basic phases of adoption, awareness, interest, evaluation, trial, and adoption seem to be evident. Both person-to-person contacts and more impersonal methods of getting information seem to influence social action. However, there appears to be some difference in the stages and the nature of their influence.

10.2 The mass media arouse interest in new ideas, methods, and projects early in the adoption process; however, interpersonal communication is especially influential in the actual decision to adopt.

Studies on diffusing new ideas to the general public appear to verify that, before being adopted, these ideas seem to move from the mass media to a group of people called "opinion leaders"; these leaders in turn confirm this information by communicating it to those who adopt it later. Information disseminated by the mass media—television, radio, newspapers, magazines, and so on—appears to serve the primary role of creating awareness about new ideas. However, later adopters—those not considered leaders—commonly consult with earlier adopters about how the new experiment went. Although large segments of a population may be exposed to a new method through the mass media, opinion leaders will usually be the first to check and compare this information against that from technical sources like scientists, commercial salespeople, and special agents. If the later adopters question information from the media, they will seek out opinion leaders to confirm or deny the aspects in doubt. Opinion leaders seem to respond more quickly to the more impersonal, mass media sources of information while the later adopters tend to rely more on the personal views of the opinion leaders. Lazarsfeld, Berelson, and Gaudet (1948) and Katz and Lazarsfeld (1955) very early described this as the two-step flow of communication. That is, information flows, in the first step, from impersonal sources like the mass media to the opinion leaders; in the second step, opinion leaders influence the nonleaders by means of word of mouth. In reality more than two steps probably occur, making adoption of innovations a multiple-step flow of influence rather than simply a two-step flow. Research, however, seems clearly to support the observation that when information is received at the stage of initial awareness, the mass media are obviously more efficient than interpersonal communication but the reverse appears true for the stage of acceptance or adoption.

Abstract

Johan Arndt, "A Test of a Two-Step Flow in Diffusion of a New Product," *Journalism Quarterly*, Vol. 45 (1968), pp. 457-465.

Arndt wanted to discover whether opinion leaders would be more affected than nonleaders by information from the mass media. He also sought answers to the following questions: Is word-of-mouth information more likely to flow from leaders to nonleaders? Do opinion leaders add to and interpret the messages received from the media? Are receivers of favorable word-of-mouth information more likely to buy the new product than receivers of unfavorable word-of-mouth information? Are later buyers more likely to receive information by word of mouth?

A new brand of a frequently purchased food product was displayed in a commissary catering solely to the residents of a 495-unit apartment complex for married students. Each wife in the complex was sent a letter from the manufacturer and a coupon allowing her to buy the product at a third of the retail price. After the expiration of a 16-day test period, personal interviews were completed with 91% of the wives. The time of purchase was determined by when the coupon was redeemed. Opinion leadership was determined by having each respondent indicate three individuals with whom she would most likely discuss new products. A distinction was made between hearing and giving comments about the product.

Among receivers of word-of-mouth information, the leaders were not more likely to buy the new product but, among those not exposed by word of mouth, they were more likely to buy. Since exposure by word of mouth actually decreased the probability of purchase among leaders, this suggests that they were more influenced by the manufacturer's letter while the nonleaders appeared to be more influenced by word of mouth. Findings support the notion of influence from impersonal sources to opinion leaders, the first step in the two-step flow. The leaders were more active participants in the word-of-mouth process as senders and receivers, but the face-to-face interaction was more characterized by opinion sharing between leaders and nonleaders than opinion seeking. Leaders voiced their own opinions of the product and the coupon offer rather than the selling point stated in the letter and the store display. This supports the hypothesis that opinion leaders play an active role by adding to or filtering mass media information in order to provide new information to the nonleaders. Of the respondents exposed to favorable word-of-mouth information, 54% purchased the product while only 18% exposed to unfavorable word-of-mouth comments made purchases. Later buyers tended to report exposure to word-of-mouth information more often than earlier buyers. Adopters were more likely than nonadopters to receive information by word of mouth.

■ Information communicated through the mass media seems to be most effective in arousing interest and creating awareness of new ideas, methods, and products. It also appears to be influential in creating change among opinion leaders. However, interpersonal communication is probably more influential in bringing about actual adoptions of new ideas, methods, and products among most members of a group. The two-step or multiple-step flow of information and influence from the media to opinion leaders to nonleaders appears to be an actuality, with the face-to-face, word-of-mouth diffusion of information being an important part of the actual adoption process.

10.3 Individuals tend to adopt new ideas at different times, but they fall into one of five time-of-adoption categories: innovators, early adopters, early majority, late majority, and laggards.

Because the adoption of new ideas, methods, and products appears over a period of time, it is not unusual to make the decision to adopt at different times. The adoption process described in proposition 10.1 anticipates that the adopter will pass through a number of stages, each of which takes some interval of time to complete. Rogers (1968) has described five adopter categories based on information from more than 5,000 different studies of innovation adoption:

1. *Early Innovators* A venturesome group of people, eager to try and adopt new ideas before others, are also willing to accept occasional failure when a new practice does not seem to work out. Early innovators appear to be in touch with other early innovators even if they are separated by geographical distances. Generally, they control substantial financial resources and are able to absorb unprofitable innovations.

2. *Late Innovators* A respected group of prestigious members of the local community or social system that usually are the opinion leaders of their community. Considered to be the people to check with about new things, they are not very far ahead of the average member of the community in innovativeness, but they represent the model upon which others build. They maintain their position in the community by making successful adoptions before others.

3. *Early Adopters* A group of individuals who usually deliberate for some time before adopting new methods—but usually do so before the average members of the community do. They also stick with the facts as they have adopted for a longer period of time than the innovators. Though they willingly adopt after others have experimented and usually interact with their peers, they rarely hold leadership positions.

4. *Late Adopters* A skeptical group who adopt new ideas after the average members of the community since they approach innovations with great caution. They must be convinced

of the value of new ways, usually forming the major part of organizational memberships without playing the most active roles. They do not participate in as many activities outside the community as people who adopt earlier.

5. *Laggards* A traditional group made up of older community members who are frankly suspicious of innovations and innovators. The last to adopt an innovation, if they ever do, they have no opinion leaders in their group and often are isolates uninterested in new ideas.

Abstract

James S. Coleman, Elihu Katz, and Herbert Mensel, "The Diffusion of an Innovation Among Physicians," *Sociometry,* Vol. 2 (Dec. 1957), pp. 253–270.

This study attempted to discover the social processes that intervened between the initial trials of a new drug by a few local innovators and its final use by virtually the entire medical community. In the experiment 125 general practitioners, internists, and pediatricians in four midwestern cities, ranging in population from 30,000 to 110,000, were interviewed. Each doctor interviewed was asked: To whom did he most often turn for advice and information? With whom did he most often discuss his cases in the course of an ordinary week? Who were the three friends among his colleagues whom he saw most often socially? Rather than ask the doctors when they first used the new drug, the authors had the prescription records of the local pharmacies checked. Three days' sampling periods at approximately monthly intervals over the 15 months following the drug's release date were used to determine when each doctor first prescribed the medication. A doctor's relative orientation to his professional colleagues and patients was inferred from his answers to the following question: How would you rank the importance of these characteristics in recognizing a good doctor in a town like this?

1. The respect in which he is held by his own patients

2. His general standing in the community

3. The recognition given him by his local colleagues

4. The research and publications he has to his credit

Doctors were classified as "profession-oriented" or "patient-oriented" according to whether 1 and 2 (patient) or 3 and 4 (profession) were generally ranked higher. The adoption behavior of pairs of doctors sociometrically related to one another were plotted on a chart.

Results showed that the profession-oriented doctors generally used the drug earlier than the patient-oriented doctors, 90% of the former having adopted the new drug by the sixth month but only 42% of the latter. Also, doctors who were mentioned by many of their colleagues when answering the sociometric questions used the drug, on the average, earlier than those named by a few or none of their colleagues. The doctors named as friends by three or more colleagues were much faster to introduce the new drugs than the rest.

■ The results clearly suggested that there may be successive stages in the diffusion of new drugs to the medical community. The first networks appeared to be those connecting the doctors in the profession relationship of advisors and discussion partners. Only then did the friendship network seem to become operative. Finally, those doctors who did not introduce the drug by six months did not seem to be influenced by their colleagues but responded instead to influences outside their social network such as retail men, ads, and journal articles. The adoption of new drugs appeared to occur so that physicians were distributed along the continuum from innovators to laggards.

10.4 The use of television advertising is a form of social action that can produce decisions leading to the sale of a product.

Television has grown faster than any other advertising medium in history. Within a 20-year period, advertising expenditures on television have risen from nothing to almost $3-billion dollars. All except $500,000 of that sum was spent by national, general advertisers, making television a leading influence in the country. In spite of some research suggesting that the mass media serve primarily to expose people to ideas, methods, and products, advertisers pay great sums because, as they say, "television has an almost unbelievable impact." Dunn (1969) states: "Witness the rapid rise of Lestoil from obscurity to leadership in its field, almost entirely through the use of spot television." Lestoil, a cleaning detergent, was advertised in newspapers, but failed to gain the market until advertised on television. Television is considered by some to be an effective and personal door-to-door sales staff, especially when the message is presented by a popular celebrity.

A number of factors influence the effectiveness of television advertising. Levitt (1970) attempted to find out what basic dimensions underlie a viewer's response to commercials. Based on a survey of both advertising and general studies related to attribute ratings, 525 descriptive words were selected for scaling commercials. Eleven commercials were shown individually to 30 respondents who were asked to check those words that applied to each commercial. The most frequently checked words were presented to the subjects accompanied by a five-point scale running from "fits extremely well" to "does not fit." Using this rating scale, a different group of ten subjects rated each of the 11 commercials. The results for each word were subjected to analysis of variance. A total of 71 words emerged as discriminating and were used in routine testing of commercials for almost a year. Based on the descriptive words selected by subjects involved in this study, it appears that lively, vigorous, exciting, and enthusiastic commercials, which are also amusing and humorous, may be more effective than other commercials. In addition, such commercials should be lovely, beautiful, tender, and sensitive. Finally, if they are helpful, worth remembering, and important for the viewer, over 90% of their effectiveness can be accounted for. It is important to remember, however, that these words describe perceptions of the viewer.

In addition to viewer perceptions of the qualities of commercials, there has been some concern about how a commercial is affected by the program in which it is inserted. Kennedy (1971) inserted commercials in natural breaks at the beginning, middle, and closing parts of a suspense thriller and a situation comedy. Results indicate that over 20% more of the viewers of a situation comedy recalled the brand name of the advertised products than did those watching the suspense thriller. Apparently program environment can affect commercial effectiveness.

The manner through which television advertising influences social action is not clearly understood. Krugman (1971) states that as far as advertising on television is concerned, ". . . persuasion as such, i.e., overcoming the resistant attitude is not involved at all and that it is a mistake to look for it in our personal lives as a test of television's advertising impact." Krugman seems to believe that, as we are bombarded with a multitude of unimportant details in television commercials, the constant repetition moves some kinds of information from our short-term memory into our long-term memory. Later, when we are looking for a product to buy, the details in our long-term memory provide a perceptual emphasis that allows us to see a product very suddenly in a new light. For example, through television advertising we may be exposed briefly to the idea that the product being sold on the screen is *modern;* thus, when we arrive at the store to make our purchase, we still see the old reliable brand we have been buying as reliable, but our decision is now based on a different perceptual emphasis, that of modernity. This new set toward modernity occurs because the television commercials were short and considered of no great importance. As a result, the viewing public lets down its psychological guard toward the repetitive commercial. Krugman suggests that television is a low-involvement experience in which gradual shifts in perceptual structure occur and are activated by the necessity to make behavioral choices at the time of purchase. He believes, then, that television advertising is effective as a tool of social action, although not in the normal sense of persuasion.

Abstract

Stephen W. Hollander and Jacob Jacoby, "Recall of Crazy, Mixed-up, TV Commercials," *Journal of Advertising Research,* Vol. 13 (June 1973), pp. 39–42.

Hollander and Jacoby attempted to determine what effect a distraction would have on recalling brand names in commercials. More specifically, they combined the audio portion of one commercial with the video portion of another and attempted to discover what effect this would have on recall of brand names. Subjects viewed the commercials and completed questionnaires, then listed all the brands of products advertised during the program.

Subjects were able to recall the names of most of the brands involved. Interestingly, the recall of brand names was higher for the split commercials than for the intact commercials; not once, in fact, did the split commercials reduce brand recall. Some superiority seemed to occur for recall of the brand appearing in the video mode.

■ The researchers suggest that being able to advertise two unrelated products simultaneously without loss in brand recall may have implications for national television advertising since two companies could combine efforts and advertise at considerable savings. One question left unanswered by the research concerns how long such novel presentations could be expected to achieve the desired results. At the present time, we are unable to explain definitely why some commercials seem to be more compelling than others. In addition, we have difficulty assessing the impact of television commercials on the buying habits of the American people. However, television commercials do seem to produce change in people. Social action, specifically demonstrated through purchase of products, does occur following television commercials. In fact, some say that television has produced significant changes in the entire buying pattern of the American consumer. If that is the case, television commercials clearly are an important factor in producing widespread social action.

Television messages can reach almost everybody in the country. Even individuals who are literate but find reading a tiresome task will spend several hours a day watching television. Although television messages may have an impact on viewers, the costs of production are great and require a creative and skillful individual to guide the creation of an effective commercial. Nevertheless, television has demonstrated its place in bringing about change in our social system.

10.5 Instigating change in social systems requires implementing a series of clearly defined steps that mark the progress of an idea from conception to implementation.

Explanations accompanying the preceding propositions have indicated both the mental steps through which individuals proceed when they accept a new idea and their characteristics as people. The question this proposition raises concerns the overall sequence of steps through which a social action campaign ought to be directed if a person or group wants to initiate some kind of social change. Beal and Bohlen (1957) have identified the dynamics of how people accept ideas. Using these constructs, they developed a model of the steps through which social change evolves. Beal (1964) modified the original statement and offered a plan for instigating social change in which "change agents deliberately guide or provoke change to occur in a social system like a community." Case and Hoffman (1969) translated the social action process described by Beal and Bohlen into a pamphlet designed to guide community development specialists in bringing about change in their areas. This model provides a system by which you should be able to construct a plan for producing social action in a social system—organization, community, city, and so on. Effective social action campaigns have been based on this outline.

Step 1: Identify Prior Social Action Programs   All social action takes place in some sort of social system—a state, county, community, church, club. Social action must, in some way, relate to at least part of one of these social systems. To work intelligently for social change, we must look at the overall social system in which the action will take place. For every social action program, there exists within the system some kind of past experience relating to the action to be undertaken. Somewhere in a community's history, for example, a similar or related program succeeded or failed, or created cooperation, a crisis, or conflict. The first step in effective social action is to identify the earlier, relevant programs and discover how they fared.

Step 2: Secure Agreement that a Problem Situation Exists in the Social System   Who or what starts social action? Usually, two or more people agree that some kind of problem or situation exists about which something needs to be done. These people may be part of the community (insiders) or they may be members of some other group (outsiders). The second step in social action is to bring about a convergence of interest on a problem. Some groups, more than others in the community, will be more interested in and affected by the problem and the plan for social action. Now is a good time to identify not only the problem but also those groups who will be particularly concerned and how they will be affected. Make a list of the groups and outline the ways in which they will be affected.

Step 3: Create Initiating Sets or Groups to Contact Others   Those people who feel something should be done about a problem must be organized into small groups or sets for the purpose of making contacts with others. Those involved in the initiating sets should feel the problem is important enough for them to be willing to start some action in its favor. Usually, these sets take the problem to the key influential individuals and groups in the community for their approval.

Step 4: Contact Legitimizers for Approval of the Idea   In almost every community, company, institution, or group, there are certain people or groups whose appproval or acceptance of proposed projects is necessary in order to make them "legitimate." Thus, legitimization is the giving of sanction by key persons or groups to new ideas so the public will accept them. The initiating sets usually contact the legitimizers and ask them to pass judgment on the proposal. If they were bypassed, legitimizers might feel their position challenged and create resistance to the action. Legitimizers may be one or two people, but sometimes they are an informal group of five or six or a formal group such as a church, the Chamber of Commerce, or a service club like the Kiwanis or Rotary. Since legitimizers usually have a reputation of accomplishment for the community, it is best to obtain their stamp of approval before an idea gets to the community's voters.

Step 5: Diffuse Information to the Public   Now is the time to take the problem beyond the initiating sets and the legitimizers. Knowledge about the problem should be made available to everyone who will be affected. Those groups of individuals who let the public know and are people with wide acquaintances are called *diffusion sets,* which, once organized, have the major task of helping members of the community define the problem as one of their own. Use of the mass media (see Chapter 6) may be very important to a diffusion set in getting information to large numbers of individuals since awareness of a new idea or problem often occurs from such exposure. Of course, the initiating sets may not necessarily be the best ones to convince others that a problem exists. What is needed here are people with outstanding abilities in interpersonal communication and persuasion.

Step 6: Obtain a Commitment to Action   Social action is more likely to be effective if the people involved have been asked to make a public commitment in support of it. Often people appear to accept an idea or recognize a problem, but fail to be sufficiently motivated to act. In social action campaigns, do not assume that agreement on an issue necessarily means willingness to act. It is essential to get a commitment from individuals to do *something.* Such commitments take the form of votes of confidence, agreements to attend meetings or act at the proper time, pledges of money, and actual participation in sets that initiate action and diffuse information. Research in persuasion has demonstrated dramatic differences between those who commit themselves and those who do not.

Step 7: Establish Goals for Individuals and Groups   Once a problem has been established and commitment obtained to act, some concrete targets or goals—along with general program aims—must be established for the relevant groups to reach to solve the problem. Specific goals should be stated in regard to the following: the ultimate objective (such as build a new sports stadium); the intermediate goals (such as raise $200,000 for the stadium's physical structure and $50,000 for its equipment); and the changes anticipated in human behavior (such as attract more business in the area of the stadium after it is finished or increase pride in having a professional hockey team).

Step 8: Decide on How to Bring about the Change   As soon as goals are established, it is important to explore alternative ways for achieving them, since those committed to social change sometimes disagree on or are unsure of the method. Assessing the consequences of each approach is therefore important; analysis of suggestions will help eliminate those with undesirable or impractical consequences. By being creative and having several of the best alternatives available, you are more likely to reach your goal.

Step 9: Devise a Formal Plan of Work   After the goals and means have been selected, the next step is to lay out a plan of work in which some very specific actions are stated or outlined in a formal way. This plan should include decisions about finances, specific tasks that the individuals involved in the social action will have to perform, the time sequence that must be followed, the committees needed to be set up, the kinds of personnel essential, the buildings required, the meetings that should be scheduled, the amount and kinds of publicity and visual materials required, and the training necessary to enable those involved to do what they are assigned.

Step 10: Mobilize the Resources   After the plan of work has been carefully stated, the resources must be brought together and organized so that this plan can be carried out. Time must be allocated to the work, people must be scheduled, physical facilities must be located and often moved to the appropriate site, finances must be set aside, and publicity prepared and disseminated. Careful attention to the mobilization of resources may help to insure that the human, physical, financial, and communication resources are actually ready to help with the project.

Step 11: Launch the Program   In order to provide the motivation for a successful social action program, the project needs to be launched. In other words, the program should be made into a big event so that people will know it is under way. Some programs do not lend themselves to a skyrocket type of launching, but some sort of special recognition should be given to the project and those who will play an important role in getting it accomplished. A fund drive, a series of tours, a big kickoff dinner, and a full-page newspaper ad are all ways of launching a program.

Step 12: Carry Out the Plan and Evaluate What Happens   Beginning the actual work for accomplishing the tasks is last. Most of the action steps correspond to those in the plan of work, but some will be continuous and others will occur sequentially. Between each of these steps, as elsewhere along the social action profile, evaluating what has been done and how well it has worked is important. However, a final or total program evaluation should also be made. Answer such questions as: Did we accomplish what we set out to do? Were the methods effective? Did we make effective use of the resources? How would we plan differently if we were to do it again? What did we learn? Where do we go from here?

Abstract

Charles R. Hoffer, "Social Action in Community Development," *Rural Sociology*, Vol. 23 (1958), pp. 43–51.

Hoffer attempted to carry out a sociological analysis of the process through which social action occurs in a community. He considered three general aspects of the action process: (1) initiation, (2) legitimization, and (3) execution of the proposed action. Using this general design for analyzing social action, Hoffer studied the manner in which social action occurred in several different communities. Basically, the study focused upon certain actions that were undertaken within each community and attempted to determine the process through which the action was finally accomplished.

Based on the analysis of these several communities, Hoffer concluded that felt needs, crises, and anticipated needs may be considered as the causal factors initiating social action. However, it does not follow that when a need is recognized the action to meet it will be forthcoming. Only when someone in the community with sufficient power, prestige, or influence makes or approves the proposal does action occur. The initiation of projects by groups or persons outside the community is likely to be unsuccessful unless they have legal authority. Principles seemingly verified in Hoffer's study is that the recognition of need alone is insufficient to produce action. The culture of the people, the nature of their social relationships, and the motives engendered by them are equally important.

After social action is proposed, the next step is legitimization or the process of making the proposed action a legitimate one for the community. The communities studied seemed to indicate that legitimization is given by a formally organized group or by a formal process such as voting. Actually, these may not always be necessary, since informal groups may possess sufficient power to oppose action not initiated or approved by them. After a program of action has been initiated and legitimized, plans for its execution must be made definite or its goals will not be achieved. In this study Hoffer found three ways by which the execution phase was accomplished, namely (1) employing an agency to do the work, (2) assigning the task to an existing organization in the community, and (3) establishing an organization especially for the task. The objectives of the action necessarily had an important influence in the selection and the method.

■ Social action is obviously a complicated process. However, a consideration of the essential aspects and steps involved in the process helps us to understand social action in a local community situation and to prevent neglecting these important elements in community development programs. To bring about social change, the initiator should focus attention on the social systems existing in the community and aim to legitimize the proposed action by including those parts of the power structure that may be affected by the proposal. Careful plans for executing the action must be made to assure that the goals will be met.

Summary

Social action is a primary way of achieving goals in a community, organization, or other social system. It involves the acceptance by individuals and groups of people of an idea or a practice and then the adoption of this different way of doing things. Social action occurs in most cases through a series of interrelated steps. These stages in the adoption process are not necessarily discrete or mutually exclusive, and persons involved in the process appear to be aware of them. Social action involves normal aspects of communication, including intrapersonal, interpersonal, and organizational communication, as well as mass media. The mass media are used largely to arouse interest in new ideas while interpersonal communication is especially influential in the actual decision to adopt. People tend to adopt new ideas at different times, falling into one of the five time-of-adoption categories discussed in this chapter. Television advertising is a particularly effective form of social action designed to produce decisions leading to the sale of a product. However, instigating change in large social systems requires implementing a series of clearly defined steps that mark the progress of an idea from conception to completion. An awareness of the process of social action will make us better able to work to achieve desirable changes in the organizations and communities to which we belong.

Background Readings

Social action is an attempt to produce change in the social order in a systematic manner. The literature on social action is probably more theoretical and anecdotal than most other areas treated in this book. Much has been done, however, in certain areas of influence such as advertising and marketing in an effort to determine what kinds of messages change people and social relations. These readings offer a touch of the enchantment of social action.

Bennis, Warren G., Kenneth D. Benne, and Robert Chin, eds., *The Planning of Change,* 2nd ed. (New York: Holt, Rinehart and Winston, 1969). This is a hefty volume that lays the foundation for understanding how change is created, implemented, evaluated, maintained, and resisted. It covers the full range of social change.

Bettinghaus, Erwin P., *Persuasive Communication* (New York: Holt, Rinehart and Winston, 1968), Chapter 11, "Persuasion and Social Action." This chapter blends the theory and practice of persuasion with the research and change notions of the social action tradition. A concise and systematic presentation of the social action process.

Crane, Edgar, *Marketing Communications* (New York: John Wiley & Sons, 1965). This is an analysis of the principles of human behavior to which the techniques of advertising, selling, public relations, and other market-oriented fields must adapt.

Hoffer, Eric, *The True Believer* (New York: Harper & Row, 1951). As the preface says, ". . . this book deals with some peculiarities common to all mass movements," whether they are called religious, social, national, or international. Written in a dynamic style, this book is one of the most interesting of its type.

Postthoughts
Communication Studies: The Future

As the popular song says, "We've only just begun." While writing his study on communication, Mortensen (1972) observed that the preparation of the book involved "a systematic review of over one hundred scientific journals, a survey of some 100,000 titles, and a working bibliography of 6,000 articles. Yet even so extensive a coverage fails to exhaust a field that only recently has come to discover the problems associated with an embarrassment of riches." With so much research related to communicative behavior available, we have obviously considered only a small portion of it. However, this consideration provides a beginning, a jumping-off place, a model to use as we move further into the study of communication in the future. We have offered, of course, no final answers. Perhaps none can be found. Hopefully, you will still be willing to seek, recognizing that the value lies more in the seeking than the finding.

Communication research over the years has blossomed from a wide variety of disciplinary sources. It has benefited from the insights of numerous scientific disciplines, including psychology, sociology, physics, biology, anthropology, political science, and, of course, speech communication. From these sources has come a vast outpouring of scientific literature. No single field has had a monopoly on insight and research related to human communication. Relevant data has come from a wide range of areas of scientific inquiry.

Undoubtedly, the diversity will continue. However, as our society becomes more and more aware of the crisis in communication and increasingly demands the assistance of communication experts in meeting this crisis, perhaps we will see a greater willingness of professionals in many fields to cross disciplinary boundaries and work together to understand what happens when individuals attempt to communicate with one another. Perhaps such a felt need will soon trigger the collective social action necessary to achieve cooperative endeavors.

Our advances in technology make almost limitless our opportunities to study communication. The availability of the computer, for example, frees the scientist from the time-consuming operations of the past and the limitations of his memory. As a tool that can rapidly provide communicologists with bibliographies, statistics, collations, cross references, frequency counts, and research models, it frees us from the routine tasks of the past for the creative, conceptual thinking necessary for the research of the future.

We cannot know what directions future research in communication will take. However, it seems apparent that it must focus on socially significant behaviors, studying communication as a complex process of interactions among messages and other variables. It also seems apparent that future research must be conducted within the context of theory development, since the study of communication depends greatly upon the strength of its theory. By theory we refer to any organized set of interrelated statements based on a coherent and reasonably well-understood set of concepts serving as a central focus to a field of study. Communicologists in the future must focus a large portion of their efforts on generating meaningful theory. Unfortunately, most past research has contributed little to theory building. Some has focused on isolated hypotheses that might make interesting reading in the Sunday supplement but do little to advance the discipline.

In addition to emphasizing the importance of building theory through our future research, we believe we must also emphasize the nature of communication as an interactive, ongoing process. We cannot view communication as something static that once known remains the same forever. Rather, it is constantly changing—and this change is always outmoding our former theories, our former propositions or, at least, making them less than completely valid. The research of the future must recognize this highly interactive nature of communication and focus upon it.

Communication research in the future will most definitely be concerned with relating various communication theories and research between fields of related disciplines. Research in linguistics, psychology, sociology, and speech communication—to name a few fields—will need to be related in future research if we are going to further our understanding of human society's most important characteristic —the ability to communicate.

Finally, hopefully, communication research in the future will attempt to extend the generalizations and propositions derived from experiments in the field to the larger society. We must find means for socially applying what we are able to learn, since the pressing problems facing us everywhere in the world are often consequences of malfunctions in communication. To discover remedies for these problems is certainly a vital goal for future research.

These few ideas represent some of our views on where we are going or may go. What has been done in the past is important for it provides the foundation upon which we can build. Some of the research is weak and must be reconsidered, perhaps replaced, although other research may stand the test of time. But most of what there is to know about how human beings communicate with one another is not yet known. Perhaps it is not knowable. However, unless we try, we will always wonder. The challenge is yours. Will you accept it?

Background Readings

The future of communication studies, like any field, derives its strength from the past. Communication is at once one of the oldest disciplines and one of the newest. What has happened illumines what will happen. These readings are both historical and futuristic.

Cherry, Colin, *On Human Communication: A Review, A Survey, and a Criticism* (New York: John Wiley & Sons, 1957), Chapter 2, "Evolution of Communication Science—An Historical Review." This chapter details the historical evolution of man as a user of language. The author traces the development of a mathematical theory of communication.

Harms, L. S., *Human Communication: The New Fundamentals* (New York: Harper & Row, 1974). The Introduction provides a space-age review of the development of communication systems, whereas Chapter 11 discusses some probable developments in technology that will influence human communication in the future, like the auviphone, man–machine tutorials, and the home communication center.

Kibler, Robert J., and Larry L. Barker, eds., *Conceptual Frontiers in Speech Communication* (New York: Speech Communication Association, 1969). This is a report of the New Orleans Conference on Research and Instructional Development of the Speech Communication Association. It contains recommendations for the future development of instruction and research in the broad fields of speech and communication.

Schramm, Wilbur, ed., *The Science of Human Communication* (New York: Basic Books, 1963). Chapter 1 is a historical review of the development of communication research in the United States.

References

Allport, Gordon, and Leo Postman, *The Psychology of Rumor* (New York: Holt, Rinehart and Winston, 1947).

Applbaum, Ronald L., Karl Anatol, Ellis R. Hays, Owen O. Jensen, Richard E. Porter, and Jerry E. Mandel, *Fundamental Concepts in Human Communication* (San Francisco: Canfield Press, 1973), p. 188.

Arndt, Johan, "A Test of a Two-Step Flow in Diffusion of a New Product," *Journalism Quarterly,* Vol. 45 (1968), pp. 457-465.

Arnold, William E., and James C. McCroskey, "Experimental Studies of Perception Distortion and the Extensional Device of Dating," paper presented at the Speech Communication Association Convention, Los Angeles, 1967.

Asch, Solomon E., "Opinions and Social Pressure," in *Small Groups: Studies in Social Interaction,* eds. A. Paul Hare, Edgar F. Borgatta, and Robert F. Bales, rev. ed. (New York: Alfred A. Knopf, 1965), pp. 318-324.

Back, Kurt W., "Influence through Social Communication," *Journal of Abnormal and Social Psychology,* Vol. 46 (1956), pp. 9-23.

Baker, Eldon E., "The Immediate Effects of Perceived Speaker Disorganization on Speaker Credibility and Audience Attitude Change in Persuasive Speaking," *Western Speech,* Vol. 29 (Summer 1965), pp. 148-161.

Baker, Eldon E., and W. Charles Redding, "The Effects of Perceived Tallness in Persuasive Speaking," *Journal of Communication,* Vol. 12 (March 1962), pp. 51-53.

Bandura, Albert, *Principles of Behavior Modification* (New York: Holt, Rinehart and Winston, 1969).

Bartlett, Frederic C., "Experiments on Remembering: The Method of Serial Reproduction," *Remembering* (London: Cambridge University Press, 1932), pp. 118-185.

Bavelas, Alex, "Communication Patterns in Task-Oriented Groups," *Journal of the Acoustical Society of America,* Vol. 22 (Nov. 1950), pp. 725-730.

Beal, George M., "Social Action: Instigated Social Change in Large Social Systems," in *Our Changing Rural Society: Perspectives and Trends,* ed. J. H. Copp (Ames, Iowa: Iowa State University Press, 1964), pp. 233-264.

Beal, George M., and Joe M. Bohlen, "The Diffusion Process," Special Report No. 18, Agricultural Extension Service, Iowa State University, March 1957.

Beal, George M., Everett M. Rogers, and Joe M. Bohlen, "Validity of the Concept of Stages in the Adoption Process," *Rural Sociology,* Vol. 22 (1957), pp. 166-168.

Berger, Emanuel M., "The Relation between Expressed Acceptance of Self and Expressed Acceptance of Others," *Journal of Abnormal and Social Psychology,* Vol. 47 (1952), pp. 778-782.

Bettinghaus, Erwin P., "The Operation of Congruity in an Oral Communication Situation," *Speech Monographs,* Vol. 28 (Aug. 1961), pp. 131-142.

Bettinghaus, Erwin P., *Persuasive Communication* (New York: Holt, Rinehart and Winston, 1973).

Biggs, Bernice P., "Construction, Validation, and Evaluation of a Diagnostic Test of Listening Effectiveness," *Speech Monographs,* Vol. 23 (March 1956), pp. 9-13.

Bloom, B. S., "Thought Processes in Lectures and Discussion," *Journal of General Education,* Vol. 7 (1953), pp. 160-169.

Boyd, Harry S., and Vernon D. Sisney, "Immediate Self-Image Confrontation and Changes in Self-Concept," *Journal of Consulting Psychology,* Vol. 31 (1967), pp. 291-294.

Brigance, W. Norwood, "How Fast Do We Talk?" *Quarterly Journal of Speech,* Vol. 12 (Nov. 1926), pp. 337-342.

Brissey, Forrest L., "The Factor of Relevance in the Serial Reproduction of Information," *Journal of Communication,* Vol. 11 (Dec. 1961), pp. 211-219.

Brissey, Forrest L., *An Experimental Technique for the Study of Human Communication* (Missoula, Mont.: University of Montana, 1964).

Brock, Timothy C., "Communicator Recipient Similarity and Decision Change," *Journal of Personality and Social Psychology,* Vol. 1 (1965), pp. 650-654.

Buckner, H. Taylor, "A Theory of Rumor Transmission," *Public Opinion Quarterly,* Vol. 29 (Spring 1965), pp. 54-55.

Burgess, Robert L., "An Experimental and Mathematical Analysis of Group Behavior within Restricted Networks," *Journal of Experimental Social Psychology,* Vol. 4 (1968), pp. 338-349.

Calvin, Allen D., "Social Reinforcement," *Journal of Social Psychology,* Vol. 56 (1962), pp. 15-19.

Carmichael, Carl W., and Gary Cronkhite, "Frustration and Language Intensity," *Speech Monographs,* Vol. 32 (1965), pp. 107-111.

Cartwright, Dorwin, "Achieving Change in People: Some Applications of Group Dynamics Theory," *Human Relations,* Vol. 4 (1954), pp. 381-392.

Case, Stuart G., and Carl J. Hoffman, "Springboards to Community Action: A Guide for Community Improvement and Resource Development," Pamphlet 18, Cooperative Extension Service, Montana State University, July 1969.

Cattell, Raymond B., ed., *Handbook of Multivariate Experimental Psychology* (Chicago: Rand-McNally & Co., 1966), p. 20.

Chorus, A., "The Basic Law of Rumor," *Journal of Abnormal and Social Psychology,* Vol. 48 (Sept. 1953), pp. 313-314.

Coleman, James S., Elihu Katz, and Herbert Mensel, "The Diffusion of an Innovation among Physicians," *Sociometry,* Vol. 2 (Dec. 1957), pp. 253-270.

Crawford, C. E., "The Correlation between College Lecture Notes and Quiz Papers," *Journal of Educational Research,* Vol. 12 (Nov. 1925), pp. 282-291.

Crawford, C. E., "Some Experimental Studies as a Result of College Note-Taking," *Journal of Educational Research,* Vol. 12 (Dec. 1925), pp. 379-386.

Cromwell, Harvey, "The Persistency of the Effect on Audience Attitude of the First versus the Second Argumentative Speech of a Series," *Speech Monographs,* Vol. 21 (Nov. 1954), pp. 280-284.

Cromwell, Harvey, "The Persistency of the Effect of Argumentative Speeches," *Quarterly Journal of Speech,* Vol. 41 (April 1955), pp. 154-158.

Dabbs, James M., Jr., and Howard Leventhal, "Effects of Varying the Recommendations in a Fear-Arousing Communication," *Journal of Personality and Social Psychology,* Vol. 4 (1966), pp. 525-531.

Darnell, Donald K., "The Relation between Sentence Order and Comprehension," *Speech Monographs,* Vol. 30 (1963), pp. 97-100.

Davis, Keith, "A Method of Studying Communication Patterns in Organizations," *Personnel Psychology,* Vol. 6 (1953), pp. 301-312.

Davis, Keith, "Management Communication and the Grapevine," *Harvard Business Review* Vol. 31 (Sept.-Oct. 1953), pp. 43-49.

Diehl, Charles F., Richard C. White, and Paul H. Satz, "Pitch Change and Comprehension," *Speech Monographs,* Vol. 28 (March 1961), pp. 65-68.

Dietrich, John D., "The Relative Effectiveness of Two Modes of Radio Delivery in Influencing Attitudes," *Speech Monographs,* Vol. 13 (1946), pp. 58-65.

Dittes, James E., and Harold H. Kelley, "Effects of Different Conditions of Acceptance upon Conformity to Group Norms," *Journal of Abnormal and Social Psychology,* Vol. 53 (1956), pp. 100-107.

Dodd, Stuart C., "Testing Message Diffusion in Controlled Experiments: Charting the Distance and Time Factors in the Interactance Hypothesis," *American Sociological Review,* Vol. 18 (Aug. 1953), pp. 410-416.

Dodd, Stuart C., "Formulas for Spreading Opinions: A Report of Controlled Experiments on Leaflet Messages in Project Revere," *Public Opinion Quarterly,* Vol. 22 (Winter 1958), pp. 537-554.

Downing, John, "Cohesiveness, Perception, and Values," *Human Relations,* Vol. 11 (1958), pp. 157-166.

Dunn, S. Watson, *Advertising: Its Role in Modern Marketing,* 2nd ed. (New York: Holt, Rinehart and Winston, 1969), p. 486.

Emmert, Philip, and William D. Brooks, eds., *Methods of Research in Communication* (Boston: Houghton Mifflin Co., 1970), pp. 70 and 105.

Ewbank, Henry L., "Studies in the Techniques of Radio Speech," *Quarterly Journal of Speech,* Vol. 18 (Nov. 1932), pp. 563-565.

Festinger, Leon, *A Theory of Cognitive Dissonance* (New York: Harper & Row, 1957).

Festinger, Leon, Stanley Schachter, and Kurt Back, *Social Pressure in Informal Groups: A Study of a Housing Project* (New York: Harper & Row, 1950).

Festinger, Leon, and John Thibaut, "Interpersonal Communication in Small Groups," *Journal of Abnormal and Social Psychology,* Vol. 46 (1951), pp. 92-99.

Freedman, William A., "A Study in Communication," *Journal of Communication,* Vol. 9 (1959), pp. 27-31.

Furbay, Albert L., "The Influence of Scattered versus Compact Seating on Audience Response," *Speech Monographs,* Vol. 32 (June 1965), pp. 144-148.

Gardner, Riley W., and Leander J. Lohrenz, "Leveling–Sharpening and Serial Reproduction of a Story," *Bulletin of the Menninger Clinic,* Vol. 24 (Nov. 1960), pp. 295-304.

Gilkinson, Howard, "Experimental and Statistical Research in General Speech: II. Speakers, Speeches, and Audiences," *Quarterly Journal of Speech,* Vol. 30 (April 1944), pp. 180-186.

Goldmark, Peter C., "Communication and the Community," *Scientific American,* Vol. 227 (Sept. 1972), pp. 143-150.

Gordon, Raymond L., "Interaction between Attitude and the Definition of the Situation and the Expression of Opinion," *American Sociological Review,* Vol. 17 (1952), pp. 50-58.

Greenberg, Bradley S., "Diffusion of News of the Kennedy Assassination," *Public Opinion Quarterly,* Vol. 28 (1964a), pp. 225-232.

Greenberg, Bradley S., "Person to Person Communication in the Diffusion of News Events," *Journalism Quarterly,* Vol. 41 (1964b), pp. 489-494.

Greenberg, Bradley S., and Gerald R. Miller, "The Effects of Low-Credible Sources on Message Acceptance—Experiment II: The Effect of Immediate versus Delayed Identification of a Low-Credible Source," *Speech Monographs,* Vol. 33 (June 1966), pp. 131-132.

Gruner, Charles R., "An Experimental Study of Satire as Persuasion," *Speech Monographs,* Vol. 32 (June 1965), pp. 149-153.

Gulley, Halbert E., and David K. Berlo, "Effect of Intercellular and Intracellular Speech Structure on Attitude Change and Learning," *Speech Monographs*, Vol. 23 (Nov. 1956), pp. 288-297.

Haiman, Franklyn, "An Experimental Study of the Effects of Ethos in Public Speaking," *Speech Monographs*, Vol. 16 (1949), pp. 190-202.

Hare, A. Paul, *Handbook of Small Group Research* (New York: The Free Press, 1962), p. 24.

Harwood, Kenneth A., "Listenability and Rate of Presentation," *Speech Monographs*, Vol. 22 (March 1955), pp. 57-59.

Hartman, George W., "A Field Experiment on the Comparative Effectiveness of 'Emotional' and 'Rational' Political Leaflets in Determining Election Results," *Journal of Abnormal and Social Psychology*, Vol. 31 (1936), pp. 99-114.

Heller, Kenneth, John B. Davis, and Roger A. Myers, "The Effects of Interviewer Style in a Standard Interview," *Journal of Consulting Psychology*, Vol. 30 (1966), pp. 501-508.

Hoffer, Charles R., "Social Action in Community Development," *Rural Sociology*, Vol. 23 (1958), pp. 43-51.

Hollander, Stephen W., and Jacob Jacoby, "Recall of Crazy, Mixed-up, TV Commercials," *Journal of Advertising Research*, Vol. 13 (June 1973), pp. 39-42.

Holzman, Philip S., and Riley W. Gardner, "Leveling and Repression," *Journal of Abnormal and Social Psychology*, Vol. 59 (Sept. 1959), pp. 151-155.

Holzman, Philip S., and Riley W. Gardner, "Leveling–Sharpening and Memory Organization," *Journal of Abnormal and Social Pschology*, Vol. 61 (Sept. 1960).

Hovland, C. I., and Walter Weiss, "The Influence of Source Credibility on Communication Effectiveness," *Public Opinion Quarterly*, Vol. 15 (1951), pp. 635-650.

Irwin, John V., and Herman H. Brockhaus, "The 'Teletalk Project': A Study of the Effectiveness of Two Public Relations Speeches," *Speech Monographs*, Vol. 30 (Nov. 1963), pp. 359-368.

Isaac, Stephen, and William B. Michael, *Handbook in Research and Evaluation* (San Diego: Robert K. Knapp, 1971), pp. 13-15.

Jahoda, Marie, "Conformity and Independence—Psychological Analysis," *Human Relations*, Vol. 12 (1959), pp. 99-120.

Janis, Irving L., and Seymour Feshbach, "Effects of Fear-Arousing Communications," *Journal of Abnormal and Social Psychology*, Vol. 48 (1953), pp. 78-92.

Johnson, David W., "Effects of the Order of Expressing Warmth and Anger on the Actor and the Listener," *Journal of Counseling Psychology*, Vol. 18 (1971), pp. 571-578.

Johnson, David W., "Effects of Warmth of Interaction, Accuracy of Understanding, and the Proposal of Compromises on Listener's Behavior," *Journal of Counseling Psychology*, Vol. 18 (1971), pp. 207-216.

Johnson, Wendell, and Carolyn B. Wood, "John Told Jim What Joe Told Him: A Study of the Process of Abstracting," *Etc.*, Vol. 2 (Autumn 1944), pp. 10-28.

Jones, Edward E., and Jane Aneshausel, "The Learning and Utilization of Contravaluent Material," *Journal of Abnormal and Social Psychology*, Vol. 53 (1956), pp. 27-33.

Jourard, Sidney M., "Self-Disclosure and Other Effective Cathexis," *Journal of Abnormal and Social Psychology*, Vol. 59 (1959), pp. 428-433.

Karlins, Marvin, and Herbert I. Abelson, *Persuasion: How Opinions and Attitudes Are Changed* (New York: Springer Publishing Co., 1970).

Katz, Elihu, "The Social Itinerary of Technical Change: Two Studies on the Diffusion of Innovation," *Human Organization*, Vol. 20 (Summer 1961), pp. 70-82.

Katz, Elihu, and Paul F. Lazarsfeld, *Personal Influence: The Part Played by People in the Flow of Mass Communication* (Glencoe, Ill.: The Free Press, 1955), p. 309.

Katz, Irwin, Judith Goldston, Melvin Cohen, and Solomon Stucker, "Need Satisfaction, Perception, and Cooperative Interaction in Married Couples," *Marriage and Family Living,* Vol. 25 (Feb. 1963), pp. 209-213.

Kennedy, John R., "How Program Environment Affects TV Commercials," *Journal of Advertising Research,* Vol. 11 (Feb. 1971), pp. 33-38.

Kiesler, Charles A., and Sarah B. Kiesler, *Conformity* (Reading, Mass.: Addison-Wesley Publishing Co., 1969), p. 2.

Knower, Franklin H., "Communicology, An Overview: Philosophy, Objectives, Content," in *The Communicative Arts and Sciences of Speech,* ed. Keith Brooks. (Columbus, Ohio: Charles E. Merrill Books, 1967), pp. 98-106.

Knower, Franklin H., David Phillips, and Fern Keoppel, "Studies in Listening to Informative Speaking," *Journal of Abnormal and Social Psychology,* Vol. 40(Jan. 1945), pp. 82-88.

Korzybski, Alfred, *Selections from Science and Sanity* (Lakeville, Conn.: The International Non-Aristotelian Library, 1948), p. 37.

Kramar, Edward J., and Thomas R. Lewis, "Comparison of Visual and Nonvisual Listening," *Journal of Communication,* Vol. 1 (Nov. 1951), pp. 16-20.

Kraus, Sydney, Elaine El-Assal, and Melvin L. DeFleur, "Fear–Threat Appeals in Mass Communications: An Apparent Contradiction," *Speech Monographs,* Vol. 33 (1966), pp. 23-29.

Krugman, Herbert E., "The Impact of Television Advertising: Learning without Involvement," in *The Process and Effects of Mass Communication,* eds. Wilbur Schramm and Donald F. Roberts, rev. ed. (Urbana: University of Illinois Press, 1971), pp. 485-494.

Larsen, Otto M., and Richard J. Hill, "Mass Media and Interpersonal Communication in the Diffusion of a News Event," *American Sociological Review,* Vol. 19 (Aug. 1954), pp. 426-433.

Lazarsfeld, Paul F., Bernard Berelson, and Hazel Gaudet, *The People's Choice,* 2nd ed. (New York: Columbia University Press, 1948).

Leavitt, Harold J., "Some Effects of Certain Communication Patterns on Group Performance," *Journal of Abnormal and Social Psychology,* Vol. 46 (1951), pp. 38-50.

Lefkowitz, Monroe, Robert R. Blake, and Jane Srygley Mouton, "Status Factors in Pedestrian Violation of Traffic Signals," *Journal of Abnormal and Social Psychology,* Vol. 51 (1955), pp. 704-706.

Levine, J. M., and G. Murphy, "The Learning and Forgetting of Controversial Material," *Journal of Abnormal and Social Psychology,* Vol. 38 (1943), pp. 507-517.

Levitt, Clark, "A Multi-Dimensional Set of Rating Scales for Television Commercials," *Journal of Applied Psychology,* Vol. 54 (1970), pp. 427-429.

Levitt, Eugene E., "A Quantitative Investigation of Individual Differences in Serial Reproduction: A Contribution to the Study of Rumor," Ph.D. dissertation, Columbia University, 1952.

Loomis, James L., "Communication, the Development of Trust, and Cooperative Behavior," *Human Relations,* Vol. 12 (1959), pp. 305-315.

Ludlum, Thomas S., "The Effects of Certain Techniques of Credibility upon Audience Attitude," *Speech Monographs,* Vol. 25 (Nov. 1958), pp. 278-284.

Marlow, David, and Kenneth J. Jergen, "Personality and Social Interaction," in *Handbook of Social Psychology,* eds. Gardner Lindsey and Elliott Aronson, 2nd ed. (Reading, Mass.: Addison-Wesley Publishing Co., 1969), Vol. 3, pp. 615-616.

McCroskey, James C., and R. Samuel Mehrley, "The Effects of Disorganization and Nonfluency on Attitude Change and Source Credibility," *Speech Monographs,* Vol. 36 (March 1969), pp. 13-21.

McGuire, William J., "The Nature of Attitudes and Attitude Change," in *Handbook of Social Psychology,* eds. Gardner Lindsey and Elliott Aronson, 2nd ed. (Reading, Mass.: Addison-Wesley Publishing Co., 1969), Vol. 3, pp. 187-194.

McKeachie, Wilbert J., "Research on Teaching at the College and University Level," in *Handbook of Research on Teaching,* ed. N. L. Gage (Chicago: Rand-McNally & Co., 1963).

Meadow, Arnold, Sidney J. Parnes, and Hayne Reese, "Influence of Brainstorming Instructions and Problem Sequence on a Creative Problem-Solving Test," *Journal of Applied Psychology,* Vol. 43 (1959), pp. 413-416.

Milgram, Stanley, "The Small World Problem," *Psychology Today,* Vol. 1 (May 1967), p. 63.

Miller, Delbert C., and William H. Form, *Industrial Sociology* (New York: Harper & Row, 1951), pp. 301-302.

Miller, George A., *Language and Communication: A Scientific and Psychological Introduction* (New York: McGraw-Hill Book Co., 1951).

Miller, Gerald R., and Murray A. Hewgill, "The Effect of Variations in Nonfluency on Audience Ratings of Source Credibility," *Quarterly Journal of Speech,* Vol. 50 (Feb. 1964), pp. 36-44.

Miller, Gerald R., and Michael McReynolds, "Male Chauvinism and Source Competence: A Research Note," *Speech Monographs,* Vol. 40 (June 1973), pp. 154-155.

Mills, Judson, "Changes in Moral Attitudes Following Temptation," *Journal of Personality,* Vol. 26 (1958), pp. 517-531.

Mills, Judson, "Opinion Change as a Function of the Communicator's Desire to Influence and Liking for the Audience," *Journal of Experimental Social Psychology,* Vol. 2 (1966), pp. 152-159.

Mills, Judson, and Elliot Aronson, "Opinion Change as a Function of a Communicator's Attractiveness and Desired Influence," *Journal of Personality and Social Psychology,* Vol. 1 (1965), pp. 173-177.

Mortensen, C. David, *Communication: The Study of Human Interaction,* (New York: McGraw-Hill Book Co., 1972), p. ix.

Mouton, Jane Srygley, Robert R. Blake, and Joseph A. Olmstead, "The Relationship Between Frequency of Yielding and the Disclosure of Personal Identity," *Journal of Personality,* Vol. 24 (1956), pp. 339-347.

Mullin, Daniel W., "An Experimental Study of Retention in Education Television," *Speech Monographs,* Vol. 24 (March 1957), pp. 31-38.

Nichols, Ralph G., and Leonard A. Stevens, "Listening to People," *Harvard Business Review,* Vol. 35 (Sept.–Oct. 1957).

Pace, R. Wayne, "The President Speaks: Curricula in Communicology," *ICA Newsletter,* Vol. 19 (1970), p. 3.

Pace, R. Wayne, and Robert R. Boren, *The Human Transaction: Facets, Functions, and Forms of Interpersonal Communication* (Glenview, Ill.: Scott, Foresman and Co., 1973), pp. 355-357.

Parker, John P., "Some Organizational Variables and Their Effect upon Comprehension," *Journal of Communication,* Vol. 12 (1962), pp. 27-32.

Peterson, Brent D., "A Study of the Reactions of a Predominantly Republican Audience to Democratic Speakers," M. A. thesis, Brigham Young University, Provo, Utah, 1968.

Peterson, Warren A., and Noel P. Gist, "Rumor and Public Opinion," *American Journal of Sociology,* Vol. 57 (Sept. 1951), pp. 159-167.

Petrie, Charles, "Informative Speaking: A Summary and Bibliography of Related Research," *Speech Monographs,* Vol. 30 (June 1963), pp. 79-91.

Pope, Benjamin, and Aron Walfe Siegman, "Interviewer Warmth," in *Studies in Dyadic Communication,* eds. A. W. Siegman and B. Pope (New York: Pergamon Press, 1972), pp. 73-80.

Powell, John, *Why Am I Afraid to Tell You Who I Am?* (Chicago: Argus Communications Co., 1969), p. 43.

Raven, Bertram H., "Social Influence of Opinions and the Communication of Related Content," *Journal of Abnormal and Social Psychology,* Vol. 58 (1959), pp. 119-128.

Reece, Michael M., and Robert M. Whitman, "Expressive Movements, Warmth, and Verbal Reinforcement," *Journal of Abnormal and Social Psychology,* Vol. 64 (1962), pp. 234-236.

Rice, Berkeley, "The High Cost of Thinking the Unthinkable," *Psychology Today,* Vol. 7 (Dec. 1973), pp. 89-93.

Roethlisberger, F. G., and William J. Dickson, *Management and the Worker* (Cambridge, Mass.: Harvard University Press, 1939), pp. 421-423.

Rogers, Everett M., *Diffusion of Innovations* (New York: The Free Press, 1962), pp. 81-105.

Rogers, Everett M., "Communication and Change," in *Proceedings of the 11th Annual Institute in Technical and Organizational Communication,* ed. F. Floyd Shoemaker (Ft. Collins, Colo.: Colorado State University, 1968), pp. 37-38.

Ruja, Harry, "Outcomes of Lectures and Discussion Procedures in Three College Courses," *Journal of Experimental Education,* Vol. 22 (June 1954), pp. 385-394.

Schachter, Stanley, "Deviation, Rejection, and Communication," *Journal of Abnormal and Social Psychology,* Vol. 46 (1951), pp. 190-207.

Schachter, Stanley, Norris Ellertson, Dorothy McBride, and Doris Gregory, "An Experimental Study of Cohesiveness and Productivity," *Human Relations,* Vol. 4 (1951), pp. 229-238.

Scheidel, Thomas M., "Sex and Persuasibility," *Speech Monographs,* Vol. 30 (Nov. 1963), pp. 353-358.

Schramm, Wilbur, ed., *The Science of Human Communication* (New York: Basic Books, 1963).

Sebald, Hans, "Limitations of Communication: Mechanisms of Image Maintenance in Form of Selective Perception, Selective Memory and Selective Distortion," *Journal of Communication,* Vol. 12 (1962), pp. 142-149.

Sereno, Kenneth K., and Gary J. Hawkins, "The Effects of Variations in Speakers Nonfluency upon Audience Ratings of Attitude toward the Speech Topic in Speaker's Credibility," *Speech Monographs,* Vol. 34 (March 1967), pp. 58-64.

Shannon, Claude E., and Warren Weaver, *The Mathematical Theory of Communication* (Urbana: University of Illinois Press, 1949), p. 9.

Sharp, Harry, Jr., and Thomas McClung, "Effects of Organization on the Speaker's Ethos," *Speech Monographs,* Vol. 33 (June 1966), pp. 182-183.

Shaw, Marvin E., "A Serial Position Effect in Social Influence on Group Decisions," *Journal of Social Psychology,* Vol. 54 (1961), pp. 83-91.

Shaw, Marvin E., *Group Dynamics: The Psychology of Small Group Behavior* (New York: McGraw-Hill Book Co., 1971), p. 259.

Sheth, Jagdish N., "Word-of-Mouth in Low-Risk Innovations," *Journal of Advertising Research,* Vol. 11 (June 1971), pp. 15-18.

Siegel, Elliot R., Gerald R. Miller, and C. Edward Wotring, "Source Credibility and Credibility Proneness: A New Relationship," *Speech Monographs,* Vol. 36 (June 1969), pp. 118-125.

Simons, Herbert W., "Persuasion and Attitude Change," in *Speech Communication Behavior: Perspectives and Principles,* eds. Larry L. Barker and Robert J. Kibler (Englewood Cliffs, N. J.: Prentice-Hall, 1971), pp. 229-230.

Smith, Val Ray, "Verbal Operant Conditioning and Response Reinforcement Contingency Awareness," M.A. thesis, University of New Mexico, August 1973.

Sutton, Harold, and Lyman W. Porter, "A Study of the Grapevine in a Governmental Organization," *Personnel Psychology,* Vol. 21 (Summer 1968), pp. 223-230.

Tannenbaum, Percy, "Effect of Serial Position on Recall of Radio and News Stories," *Journalism Quarterly*, Vol. 31 (1954), pp. 319-323.

Thibaut, John W., and John Coules, "The Role of Communication in the Reduction of Interpersonal Hostility," *Journal of Abnormal and Social Psychology*, Vol. 47 (1952), pp. 770-777.

Thistlethwaite, Donald, Joseph Kemenetzky, and Hans Schmidt, "Factors Influencing Attitude Change through Refutative Communications," *Speech Monographs*, Vol. 23 (Mar. 1956), pp. 14-25.

Thompson, Ernest, "An Experimental Investigation of the Relative Effectiveness of Organizational Structure in Oral Communication," *Southern Speech Journal*, Vol. 26 (Fall 1960).

Thompson, Wayne N., *Quantitative Research in Public Address and Communication* (New York: Random House, 1967).

Thorndyke, Robert L., "The Effect of Discussion upon the Correctness of Group Decisions on the Fact of Majority Influences Allowed For," *Journal of Social Psychology*, Vol. 9 (1938), pp. 343-362.

Toffler, Alvin, *Future Shock* (New York: Bantam Books, 1970), p. 17.

Tompkins, Phillip K., and Larry A. Samovar, "An Experimental Study of the Effects of Credibility on the Comprehension of Content," *Speech Monographs*, Vol. 31 (June 1964), pp. 120-123.

Travers, Jeffrey, and Stanley Milgram, "An Experimental Study of the Small World Problem," *Sociometry*, Vol. 32 (Dec. 1969), pp. 425-432.

Treneman, Joseph, "Understanding Radio Talks," *Quarterly Journal of Speech*, Vol. 37 (April 1951), pp. 173-178.

Truax, Charles B., Ronald G. Wargo, Jerome D. Frank, and others, "Therapist Empathy, Genuineness, and Warmth and Patient Therapeutic Outcome," *"Journal of Consulting Psychology*, Vol. 30 (1966), pp. 395-401.

Ulrich, John Holway, "An Experimental Study of the Acquisition of Information from Three Types of Recorded Television Presentations," *Speech Monographs*, Vol. 24 (March 1957), pp. 39-45.

Vohs, John L., "An Empirical Approach to the Concept of Attention," *Speech Monographs*, Vol. 31 (Aug. 1964), pp. 355-360.

Wallach, Michael A., Nathan Kogan, and Daryl J. Bem, "Group Influence on Individual Risk Taking," *Journal of Abnormal and Social Psychology*, Vol. 65 (1962), pp. 75-86.

Walster, Elaine, Elliot Aronson, and Darcy Abrahams, "On Increasing the Persuasiveness of a Low Prestige Communicator," *Journal of Experimental Social Psychology*, Vol. 2 (1966), pp. 325-342.

Weiss, Walter, "Opinion Congruence with a Negative Source on One Issue as a Factor Influencing Agreement on Another Issue," *Journal of Abnormal and Social Psychology*, Vol. 54 (1957), pp. 180-186.

Weiss, Walter, "Emotional Arousal and Attitude Change," *Psychological Reports*, Vol. 6 (1960), pp. 267-280.

Whittaker, James, "Sex Differences and Susceptability to Interpersonal Persuasion," *Journal of Social Psychology*, Vol. 66 (1965), pp. 91-94.

Wilke, Walter H., "An Experimental Comparison of the Speech, the Radio, and the Printed Page as Propaganda Devices," *Archives of Psychology*, Vol. 25 (June 1934), pp. 1-32.

Windes, Russel R., Jr., "A Study of Effective and Ineffective Presidential Campaign Speaking," *Speech Monographs*, Vol. 28 (March 1961), pp. 39-49.

Worthy, Morgan, Albert L. Geary, and Gay M. Kahn, "Self-Disclosure as an Exchange Process," *Journal of Personality and Social Psychology*, Vol. 13 (1969), pp. 59-63.

Wright, Paul H., "Attitude Change under Direct and Indirect Interpersonal Influence," *Human Relations*, Vol. 19 (May 1966), pp. 199-211.

Index of Names

Dunn, S. Watson, 122

Ehninger, Douglas, 69, 102
El-Assal, Elaine, 54
Ellertson, Norris, 105
Ewbank, Henry L., 41, 68

Feshbach, Seymour, 54
Festinger, Leon, 45, 83, 104, 108
Form, William H., 107
Frank, Jerome D., 17
Freedman, William A., 49
Frey, Frederick W., 81
Furbay, Albert L., 58

Gardner, Riley W., 88
Gaudet, Hazel, 119
Geary, Albert L., 16
Gilkinson, Howard, 65
Gist, Noel P., 77
Goldhaber, Gerald M., 34, 89
Goldmark, Peter C., 71
Goldston, Judith, 22
Gordon, Raymond L., 110
Greenberg, Bradley S., 73, 98
Gregory, Doris, 105
Griffin, Kim, 33, 114
Gruner, Charles R., 58
Gulley, Halbert E., 66

Haiman, Franklyn, 94
Hare, A. Paul, 106
Harms, L. S., 131
Harrison, Randall P., 47
Hartman, George W., 51
Harwood, Kenneth A., 38
Hawkins, Gary J., 96
Hegstrom, Timothy B., 82
Heller, Kenneth, 31
Hewgill, Murray A., 96
Hill, Richard J., 74
Hitler, Adolf, 65
Hoffer, Charles R., 126
Hoffer, Eric, 128
Hoffman, Carl J., 124
Hollander, Stephen W., 123
Holtzman, Paul D., 60
Holzman, Philip S., 88
Hovland, C. I., 94, 102
Howell, William S., 69

Ingham, Harry, 23
Irwin, John V., 58, 66
Isaac, Stephen, 6, 7

Jacobson, Wally, 114
Jacoby, Jacob, 123
Jahoda, Marie, 104
Janis, Irving L., 54, 102
Jergen, Kenneth J., 104
Johnson, David W., 18, 28, 33
Johnson, Wendell, 88
Jones, Edward E., 42
Jourard, Sidney M., 27

Kahn, Gay M., 16
Kahn, Robert L., 81
Karlins, Marvin, 51, 52, 91, 102
Katz, Daniel, 81
Katz, Elihu, 117, 119, 121
Katz, Irwin, 22
Kelley, Harold H., 104
Keltner, John W., 33
Kemenetzky, Joseph, 66
Kennedy, John R., 122
Kennedy, Robert F., 55
Keoppel, Fern, 67, 68
Kibler, Robert J., 11, 131
Kiesler, Charles A., 104, 114
Kiesler, Sara B., 104, 114
Kline, F. Gerald, 11
Knapp, Mark L., 47
Knower, Franklin H., 1, 67, 68
Kogan, Nathan, 111
Korzybski, Alfred, 13
Kramar, Edward J., 68
Kraus, Sydney, 54
Krugman, Herbert E., 122

Larsen, Otto M., 74
LaRusso, Dominick, 60
Lazarsfeld, Paul F., 119
Leavitt, Harold J., 79
Lefkowitz, Monroe, 106
Leventhal, Howard, 54
Levine, J. M., 44
Levitt, Clark, 122
Levitt, Eugene E., 87
Lewis, Thomas R., 68
Lohrenz, Leander J., 88
Loomis, James L., 21
Ludlum, Thomas S., 66
Luft, Joseph, 23

Maccoby, Nathan, 81
Marlow, David, 104
Martin, Howard H., 11
McBride, Dorothy, 105
McClung, Thomas, 96
McCroskey, James S., 44, 96
McGuire, William J., 100
McKeachie, Wilbert J., 42, 64
McReynolds, Michael, 100
Meadow, Arnold, 113
Mehrabian, Albert, 47
Mehrley, R. Samuel, 96
Mensel, Herbert, 121
Michael, William B., 6, 7
Miller, Delbert C., 107
Miller, George A., 2, 81
Miller, Gerald R., 6, 95, 96, 98, 100, 102
Milgram, Stanley, 72
Mills, Glen E., 60
Mills, Judson, 45, 101
Monroe, Alan H., 69
Mortensen, C. David, 129
Mouton, Jane S., 106, 110
Mullin, Daniel W., 40
Murphy, G., 44
Myers, Roger A., 31

Nichols, Ralph G., 38

Olbricht, Thomas H., 69
Olmstead, Joseph A., 110

Pace, R. Wayne, 1, 33, 34, 86, 89
Parker, Edwin B., 81
Parker, John P., 50
Parnes, Sidney J., 113
Patton, Bobby R., 33, 114
Peterson, Brent D., 33, 34, 56, 89
Peterson, Warren A., 77
Petrie, Charles, 49
Phillips, David, 67, 68
Pool, Ithiel de Sola, 81
Pope, Benjamin, 30
Porter, Lyman W., 83
Postman, Leo, 85
Powell, John, 13
Purkey, William W., 23

Radcliffe, Terrence R., 33
Raven, Bertram H., 110
Redding, W. Charles, 6, 89, 99
Reece, Michael M., 26

Reese, Hayne, 113
Rice, Berkeley, 107
Ried, Paul E., 11
Roethlisberger, F. G., 107
Rogers, Carl R., 24
Rogers, Everett M., 61, 116, 117, 120
Rogge, Edward, 69
Rosenfeld, Lawrence B., 114
Ruja, Harry, 64

Samovar, Larry A., 64
Satz, Paul H., 57
Schachter, Stanley, 83, 104, 105, 108
Scheidel, Thomas M., 99
Schein, Edgar H., 23
Schmidt, Hans, 66
Schramm, Wilbur, 2, 81, 131
Schutz, William C., 24
Sebald, Hans, 44
Sereno, Kenneth K., 96, 114
Shannon, Claude E., 61
Sharp, Harry, Jr., 96
Shaw, Marvin E., 53
Sheth, Jagdish N., 75
Siegel, Elliot R., 95
Siegman, Aron Walfe, 30
Simons, Herbert W., 93
Sisney, Vernon D., 32
Smith, Val Ray, 93
Sondel, Bess, 47
Steele, Fred I., 23
Steiner, Gary A., 11
Stevens, Leonard A., 38
Stucker, Solomon, 22
Sutton, Harold, 83

Tannenbaum, Percy, 53
Thibaut, John W., 20, 108
Thistlethwaite, Donald, 66
Thompson, Ernest, 50
Thompson, Wayne N., 12, 38, 39, 50, 57, 67
Thorndyke, Robert L., 106
Tichenor, Phillip J., 11
Toffler, Alvin, 117
Tompkins, Phillip K., 64
Travers, Jeffrey, 72
Travers, Robert M. W., 47
Treneman, Joseph, 49
Truax, C. B., 17

Ulrich, John Holway, 41, 68

Index of Subjects

Public speaking, 63
    attitude change, 65, 66
    credibility, 66
    discussion methods, 64
    gestures, 68
    reinforcement, 67
    retention of ideas, 67, 68
    visual aids, 68

Reinforcement, 67
    theories, 21, 42, 43
Relationships, 3, 13, 16, 25
Relevant responses, 28
Research, 1, 6
Retention of ideas, 41, 42, 67, 68
Risk taking, 111
Rumor, 75, 77, 83
    ambiguity, 83
    channels, 83
    psychology of, 85
    relevance, 85
    speed, 83

Schematizing test, 88
Scientific research, 6
Security, 21
Self-concept, 32
Self-disclosure, 16, 21, 26, 27
Self-image, 32
Serial communication, 15, 82

Serial groups, 82
    correctives, 86
    distortions, 84, 88
    information, 82, 87
    rumor, 83
Serial reproduction of information, 82, 87
Similarity, 101
Sleeper effect, 97
Small group factors, 103
Social action, 115, 124, 126
Social groups, 70
Speaker influence, 94
Symbols, 3

Telephone, 70, 71
Television:
    cable, 71
    advertising, 122
    commercials, 123
Temptation, 45, 46
Trust, 21, 22
Trustworthiness, 94

Understanding, 28, 41

Values, 43, 45
Verbal reinforcement, 26
Visual aids, 68

Warmth, 18, 26